MASTER OF ME

MASTER OF ME

The Secret to Controlling Your Narrative

Keke Palmer

FLATIRON
BOOKS
NEW YORK

MASTER OF ME. Copyright © 2024 by Keke Palmer. All rights reserved. Printed in the United States of America. For information, address Flatiron Books, 120 Broadway, New York, NY 10271. EU Representative: Macmillan Publishers Ireland Ltd., 1st Floor, The Liffey Trust Centre, 117–126 Sheriff Street Upper, Dublin 1, D01 YC43.

www.flatironbooks.com

Grateful acknowledgment is made for permission to reproduce from the following:

Baby, This Is Keke Palmer: "Who Are You Really?"; "Building a Media Empire"; and "The Shifting Narrative of Black Experience." Full podcasts on Wondery+, YouTube, or wherever you get your podcasts.

Definitions and idiom definitions from Dictionary.com Unabridged, based on the Random House Unabridged Dictionary, © Random House, Inc. 2023.

Photographs of author © Dalvin Adams

Key © Arcady / Shutterstock
Comics on pages 1, 61, and 143 © Cartoon Resource / Shutterstock
Comic on page 244 © Paul Schwartzman / *The Washington Post* via Getty Images

All emojis designed by OpenMoji—the open-source emoji and icon project. License: CC BY-SA 4.0

The Library of Congress has cataloged the hardcover edition as follows:

Names: Palmer, Keke, author.
Title: Master of me : the secret to controlling your narrative / Keke Palmer.
Description: First edition. | New York : Flatiron Books, 2024.
Identifiers: LCCN 2024033382 | ISBN 9781250372512 (hardcover) | ISBN 9781250372505 (ebook)
Subjects: LCSH: Palmer, Keke. | Actresses—United States—Biography. | Singers—United States—Biography. | African American actresses—Biography.
Classification: LCC PN2287.P2245 A3 2024 | DDC 791.4302/8092 [B]— dc23/eng/20240729
LC record available at https://lccn.loc.gov/2024033382

ISBN 978-1-250-37249-9 (trade paperback)

The publisher of this book does not authorize the use or reproduction of any part of this book in any manner for the purpose of training artificial intelligence technologies or systems. The publisher of this book expressly reserves this book from the Text and Data Mining exception in accordance with Article 4(3) of the European Union Digital Single Market Directive 2019/790.

Our books may be purchased in bulk for specialty retail/wholesale, literacy, corporate/premium, educational, and subscription box use. Please contact MacmillanSpecialMarkets@macmillan.com.

First Flatiron Books Paperback Edition: 2025

10 9 8 7 6 5 4 3 2 1

I dedicate this book to my son,
and the person I became because of him.

CONTENTS

Introduction　　xi

PART I: PERFORMANCE

　　Podcast Clip: Who Are You Really? with Amy Poehler　　3

1. Who Is Pulling Your Strings?　　5
2. Tuning Out the Noise　　21
3. The Freedom to Say No　　35
4. Freak the Systems at Large　　45
5. Public Service Announcement　　51

　　Master of Me Self-Assessment Exercise　　57

PART II: POWER

　　Podcast Clip: Building a Media Empire with Tyler Perry　　63

6. Ain't That 'Bout a Bitch?　　69
7. America, We Have a Problem　　83
8. The Power of Parenthood　　93
9. Understand Your Self-Worth　　101
10. Power Dynamics　　107
11. For My Entrepreneur Baddies　　115

CONTENTS

12. A Weird, Random Moment from Set	119
13. The Darkness Will Actually Help You	123
14. I Really Do Hate Misogynoir	129
15. Affirmations for Keke (and Anyone Else Who Needs to Hear This)	133
Master of Me Self-Assessment Exercise	139

PART III: PURPOSE

Podcast Clip: The Shifting Narrative of Black Experience with Justin Simien	145
16. A Reminder	147
17. Leo	149
18. Emerald Haywood	157
19. Reframing Your Mind	163
20. A Student of Life	171
21. I Forgive You. And I Forgive Myself.	173
22. Big Boss	177
23. It's All About Patience	179
24. The First Monday in May	183
25. I'm Blessed to Do This	193
26. Keys to the Culture	201
27. Not a Momager, a Boss	207
28. She Ain't No Diva	211
29. Keep Living	221
30. Jack of All Trades, Master of Me	227
Master of Me Self-Assessment Exercise	237

Acknowledgments 241

I have always been an observer of myself.
For years, at the mercy of others. Not anymore.

INTRODUCTION

Here is a woman. Her name is Lauren but, to the world, she goes by Keke. Keke loves to perform. She can do it all, honey. She acts. She sings. She hosts. She creates. Keke has a vision for the life she wants to live. (She's a Virgo—didn't you know?) She loves her family. She loves her friends. She loves herself. And she loves God. See how Keke smiles? She is very happy.

Here is Keke's family: Mother, Father, Older Sister, Twin Sister, and Twin Brother. Mother makes sure Keke's calendar is organized and filled to the brim. Father shares scriptures and encouraging quotes in the family's group chat. Older Sister shows patience and modest wisdom. Twin Sister borrows Keke's clothes from movie sets. Twin Brother reminds Keke she'll always just be his sister. Keke's family is a circle of support, traveling from the suburbs of Chicago

INTRODUCTION

to California to watch her dreams come true. See how they stick by Keke's side? They love her.

Here is a man. He has a wonderful sense of humor and deep brown eyes. He makes Keke laugh and puts butterflies in the deepest parts of her body. Keke loves the man. The man loves Keke. Together they have a baby. Keke's purpose expands to include Baby's happiness. She works smarter, harder, and longer hours to give Baby the life he deserves. See how Baby coos for Keke? He loves her. He is very happy.

Here is Keke again. She wants to do it all (and to be clear—she *can* do it all). But she is also a human. Sometimes she feels tired. Sometimes she feels misunderstood. Sometimes she just feels like she doesn't belong. Then there are the videos, the clickbait headlines, the comments underneath her pictures—digital footprints she can't erase. She's embarrassed. She's annoyed. She cries. She hides. She takes time to herself, for herself. And the gag is that even though Keke is in the dark, she's still putting in that work. Behind closed doors, she redirects her anger. She harnesses the power she's spent years cultivating. She takes control of the narrative—her narrative—one chapter at a time. And she wants to share her lessons and these tools with you, too.

Maybe you'll value these lessons and put them into practice, or maybe you won't. And that's totally okay.

Either way, turn the page. See Keke shine.

"It goes back to being pulled out of the hat."

Part I
PERFORMANCE

[phonetic: per-**fawr**-m*uh*ns]

noun

1. a musical, dramatic, or other entertainment presented before an audience.
2. the act of <u>performing</u> a ceremony, play, piece of music, etc.
3. the execution or accomplishment of work, acts, feats, etc.
4. a particular action, deed, or proceeding.
5. an action or proceeding of an unusual or spectacular kind:
   > *His temper tantrum was quite a performance.*
6. the act of <u>performing</u>.
7. the manner in which or the efficiency with which something reacts or fulfills its intended purpose.[1]

---

1 "performance," *Dictionary.com*, 2024, https://www.dictionary.com.

> **PODCAST CLIP: WHO ARE YOU REALLY?
> WITH AMY POEHLER**

Keke Palmer: As I'm getting older, I actually find myself being like, well, you got it. I almost think more—feel more validated in my working hard and feeling like that's what I owe.

You know, I have the freedom I have now because of all the work that I put in in my early years. And so I'm not sure how I even feel and want to respond to that whole productivity thing in, in the world, because I do feel there's something to be said about it. However, there is a reality where the lack of productivity and just kind of, you know, flowing through—yeah, sometimes that does get you what you want as well.

Amy Poehler: I know, it's—that's why I love that, I love the, the riddle because the, the part of me that likes to get things done has served me so well. It's given, it's given me everything that I feel like I have. So I don't want to, um, reject that part of me. And I, and I want to thank that part of me.

I just wonder now if I want that part of me to always be running the show, because the what-I-do part is, am I what I do? Like, that's the question.

1

WHO IS PULLING YOUR STRINGS?

The truth is this: I never really wanted to be a *performer*, but I always wanted to make people feel something deeply. For me, the essence of the human experience lies in emotions—the capacity to feel, to connect, and to empathize. In my mind it's the only true reason we are here. Otherwise, we'd just be a floating spirit untethered from the ideas of self, emotion, and understanding, but I digress. What I'm saying is, none of us know why we are here, and that's scary. We have an idea, whether spiritual or scientific, but the *why* is still unknown, so we reflect on these reasons. All the while, we're navigating life's intense experiences, which take us on a wild, emotional ride—from happiness to sadness and everywhere in between—as we try to make sense of it all. In my search for answers I've noticed a trend across generations: this reluctance to embrace how those questions and our collective uncertainty make us feel. As if the coolest person is the one who doesn't give a damn, the one who remains indifferent all the time. But it's silly because we all have emotions, no matter how challenging they can be to process. Dissonance is isolating, while facing them head-on is where the true magic happens—the sweet spot where pain makes way for connection and community. This outlook on the human experience has not only informed my work but creates the drive for it. As I've grown in my craft, I've come to realize that my true gift lies in tapping into this emotional resonance and sharing it with others. In acting, I've found that taking on a character's perspective without judgment and stepping into their shoes has given me the permission and freedom to explore emotions I might not have been able to access as myself. Through this process, I've gained a deeper understanding of human emotions, which has enabled me to support others with more courage and empathy. By performing, I help others access places they never knew they needed to reach—a truly rewarding experience. It brings me immense joy to facilitate in the journey of self-discovery, and I've been fortunate enough to recognize my talent for it from a young age—a spark that's only grown stronger with time.

My parents weren't always present because they were busy being adults, obvi! And as a parent myself, I'm constantly learning that adulthood and the well-being of a tiny human being (or really being a provider to anyone other than yourself) come with a lot of responsibilities. Not to say that I felt invisible when I was younger. I did notice my parents were really engaged whenever my siblings and I were talking about creative stuff, like recent movies that we watched or new music that we just discovered that they already knew of. We'd have conversations about the Temptations, down to reciting the lines from the days-long TV special: "Ain't nobody coming to see you, Otis!" Or we'd cry watching Fantasia's winning performance on *American Idol*. My goodness, Lawrence Hilton-Jacobs's acting in *Cooley High* almost made up for how mad he made us when playing Joe Jackson in *The Jacksons: An American Dream*. It was all the hours spent watching that movie that birthed my Angela Bassett impression. Those moments with my family fueled my own creativity. And it was so cathartic to realize that a thirty-minute show or a ninety-minute movie were not solely for entertainment purposes; they also allowed me to confront more serious topics in my own life.

When I was young, something happened to me that I couldn't understand. I didn't have the language to describe it, but I felt an overwhelming sense of violation. My parents struggled to find the words to address what had happened to me. But then, while watching an episode of *Law & Order: Special Victims Unit*, we saw a story that explored the impact of childhood abuse—in the story it was a child who had endured sexual abuse by his piano teacher. That child then became an adult and repeated the same behavior with his now adolescent students. This moment marked a turning point in my understanding of the impact of media on our lives and the ways in which creative works can provide a framework for navigating complex emotions and experiences. As I reflected on this experience, I realized that being violated at a young age is traumatic. It also warps your idea of what is normal and acceptable. This turning point taught me two valuable lessons: that I wasn't alone in my experience and that my feelings were valid. This was a relief; it allowed me to see that what I was speaking to wasn't considered taboo or irrational.

It also taught me who I *didn't* want to be—which I think people forget is just as important. India Arie sang, "I am not my hair," and the words I want to sing are, "I am not my trauma." I knew I wanted to be in control of my future as much as the next person.

And so much of that is contingent upon the work we do to understand the damage that's been done, even though we have survived it. That's the thing. When we survive things, we assume that means we got out of Dodge, but hold on, Caravan! Whenever a car crashes, it doesn't matter if the engine is roaring; there is still all this debris that must be cleaned up before you can move forward. There are a million and one possibilities for survivors of traumatic events, and the reality is how we get through it and come out of it on the other side matters. Our response can mold and shape the trajectory of our entire lives. And it's especially hard when we don't have the proper resources (institutional or not) to get to the versions of ourselves that we want to be. I knew there was power in art and performance before I watched that *Law & Order: SVU* episode, but that moment validated my own feelings. And while it didn't entirely heal my inner wounds all at once, it acknowledged where I was hurting and made me feel seen. If the actors in Dick Wolf's legal drama could plant that seed for a six-year-old child, I could only imagine the ways art could be of service and how many others could use it as an emotional icebreaker. For as long as I can remember, I've always admired this profession and the professionals who constantly choose to do this work with extreme grace.

And the revelations continue to happen even to this day. The other day I was watching this movie from 2018 called *The Tale* (warning: slight spoiler ahead, so if this is on your watch list, you can go ahead and stream it, but viewer discretion is advised). In the movie, the main character, Jennifer, aka Jenny, played by Laura Dern, is in her forties (maybe even her fifties; she looks FAB! Plus fine-ass Common plays her BF, whew!) and reflecting on the relationship she'd had with an older man as a teen. At the time of these flashbacks, she's supposed to be thirteen, but you can tell that the actual actor who's supposed to play her young self looks a bit older. The idea is that Jenny is misremembering her adolescence, still trying to piece the past together. But twenty minutes into the movie, there's this switcheroo and the director makes this intentional and very impactful choice to change the original young Jenny we thought we'd be following. Her mother, played by Ellen Burstyn, is basically going through old photos with Jenny like, "No, you didn't look like that, you looked like this." She points to a picture of thirteen-year-old Jenny in a photo album that no longer looks like a movie thirteen but looks like a real, prepubescent thirteen. The scenes that the audience had witnessed up to then are re-shot with this younger girl, played by Isabelle Nélisse, at the core of these traumatic events. Once this happens, it is practically unbearable to watch—which is the point. It's a genius and innovative move on the director's end, but it's devastating to watch as an audience member.

This movie triggered me, and I found myself reflecting on my own teenage years when I was in a relationship with a twenty-year-old man at the age of fifteen. Because in my mind at the time, it seemed appropriate. Our minds do this interesting thing where, even as we grow, our ideas of certain things will stay the same unless we look back and force our current perspective to observe the past, in hindsight. It's crazy how we can reframe moments like these in order to keep one foot in front of the other, in order to survive. There's that amazing survival instinct again that gets you through the hardship by kind of dampening its intensity, but you still need that Aquaphor for the third-degree burn you forgot you had! In the same way Laura Dern's character reframed the entire event to make it seem like she was older and wiser, I also reframed my actions at the time. I was making what I considered "Big Girl Money" and felt comfortable in the driver's seat of my life. But, if I'm being honest, when I think about those formative years, I also have to consider my attitude and outlook towards life. To be real, I was in a very vulnerable place. I stayed with this person until I was about twenty and struggled emotionally. The power dynamic put me in a place that harmed me in ways I couldn't have known. I didn't have the language or the strength to accept that who he met was a child, not the woman I wanted to become.

My parents couldn't object to what they didn't know about. And by the time they knew about our relationship, I had a level of freedom that would allow me to do what I wanted regardless. They would have had to assume I was lying to them all the time—which I often was—to meet up with him. In reality, young people find ways to assert their autonomy, especially when they have the means to do so. I think my parents opted to speak to me and get the truth so that they could stay close to the situation; it's the classic case of keeping your friends close, but your enemies closer. But I don't think there was a way for them to manage it any better than anyone who has experienced something similar. When your children are growing and learning and trying to step into their own independence, you can only lock them in a cage for so long. When I was tired of the relationship and was ready to walk away, they were the first ones I told.

Now I can say with my whole chest, "Keke girl, this grown man fully took advantage of you in every way possible. He used your youth as an opportunity to groom you into someone who could benefit him. With no regard and no respect for the chance you had to become your own person and experience the ages between fifteen and twenty individually." Even ten years later, I am still understanding, unlearning, and healing from the impact that relationship had on me.

It's wild that a movie that came out only a few years ago brought me back fifteen years, back to a place I subconsciously sought to suppress. Who knew that over a business dinner with Amy Poehler, I'd get a movie reference that would allow me to tap into something that existed within me, within my past? Honestly, she probably did, because she's a Virgo and we are deep like that. I'm kidding! But seriously, that's the power of art. As much as I've always loved to entertain, that love was rooted in my parents, wanting them to be present and engaged. Which is just an artistic expression of my deep desire to make people embrace the good, the bad, and the ugly—so they, too, can feel alive, because without doing that you might as well not be living but existing. That's how performance became a useful tool for me. I want to help people find joy in difficult circumstances, confront the parts of themselves they might be trying to hide, and find connection in the shared human experience. When I'm able to do that, it feels like a spark of magic happens—like we're all suddenly more alive, more connected, and more human.

Whether I'm writing or sharing my own story or performing something like a romance, comedy, or tragedy, I have compassion for the characters I embody and the real people who've lived these extraordinary lives. At the end of the day, we are all living our own unique lives, and we're all trying to make it and get through our circumstances. I just think there's so much beauty in the understanding of how life is always continuing at this steady pace where we're all the authors of our own stories. Ever sat on a bench in the park, watching the world go by? I find myself doing it everywhere, at the gym, on the beach. It's like a real-life soap opera in my mind. Turn your head, and you'll catch a group of friends cracking up, sharing secrets, and spilling tea (and you're low-key trying to eavesdrop). Nearby, a community group is slack-roping (yep, that's a thing!), while a sun worshipper is soaking up the rays in an itsy-bitsy bikini, wondering if that text will ever come through (same, girl, same). All around us, another story is being written, another plot is thickening. Everybody is the main character in their own storyline, including you. And in that moment, it's a humbling reminder that we're all connected, different threads in the same tapestry.

When I indulge in existential thoughts (which is, like, often. Hehe), my mind drifts to fascinating stories like the *Titanic*. Beyond its tragic fate, I wonder: How many love stories unfolded on that ship? How many immigrants were seeking a new beginning? What secrets would the lives lost and the survivors' tales reveal? (And let's skip the debate about Rose and Jack's door—we all know the truth!) Anyway, I have so much gratitude for the experiences of others that inform my way of thinking. I'm passionate about bringing characters to life and serving their stories. When the cameras roll, I aim to tap into the essence of those experiences and honor them.

As I strive to be in service to the stories I tell and the experiences I have while the cameras roll, I find inspiration in the words of legendary performer and activist Josephine Baker. In a 1971 interview with journalist Erik Bye, she shared her profound approach to her craft and humanity. Erik recounts a moment when people were struck by her presence, saying, "You do something.... You make people happy." Josephine is resolute in her response: "I've never tried to make a business of making people happy. I've always tried to touch the sensibility of each human being. And I've always tried to find their good point because I believe that every human being on this earth has something good in them. . . . And I think that human beings, in general, if they have the opportunity or possibility, they can be extremely good." I find solace in her words, reminded of the power of empathy and compassion in storytelling. There is a lot more I could share about her, but I'll save that for another chapter!

I fully agree with Josephine. At the same time, I am also aware that it's not my sole duty on this earth to make every single person around me process their own feelings through the work I've created. I mean, I should say that I'm aware and learning how to consistently put that into practice. It's incredibly impossible and exhausting, and now I have a little boy who's teething and taking tiny steps. But well before Leo Beo, I'd had experiences that tested this awareness. Just like you, I'm sure, I've encountered people who resist joy, just hell-bent on not having laughter in their lives. And whenever I would bring laughter, I'd attach a sense of validation to our relationship and consider it a good thing. Until it became a bad thing for me.

When I was younger, my mother passed down her theater expertise to me, which I'll forever be grateful for. In theater you're doing a little bit of everything—singing, dancing, acting. In some cases, like with Sammy Davis Jr., you may be a host and have a one-man or one-woman show. It's just you, the stage, and the audience. My mother, Sharon, was a huge fan of Judy Garland. She revered her, reading all her books and following her career closely. I've watched her portrayal of Dorothy Gale in *The Wizard of Oz* once or twice but I've heard the stories of her personal climb to fame more times than I can count. But my mother was a true stan; she never failed to point out whenever there was a new movie, book, or documentary coming out about Judy.

I can hear Sharon now: "Look at how she's speaking with her eyes, without lines. That's not as easy as it looks, she has depth, a true entertainer." She would speak about her with so much veneration it made me want to make someone feel as inspired as my mother was by Judy.

Building on this inspiration, my mother's guidance taught me to embrace my own versatility and creativity. With her support, I never felt like I had to be or do one thing, no matter who was pressuring me to stay in one lane (and trust me, people have *tried*). In fact, one of the earliest lessons I learned from my mother was to find a way to incorporate all my skills even if the people on the other side of the table were only looking for one. I would use every trick I had in my talent bag and try to surprise the casting directors; how else was I supposed to stand out from other people auditioning in the same room?

People might read this and think, "Oh, Keke, you were just doing the most!" And I was! But look at where "doing the most" got me. The same spirit that drove my mother to celebrate talents like Judy Garland, who defied categorization, is what I want to pass on to you: don't be afraid to bring all your talents to the table, because the only thing too much is the limitations we place on ourselves. I'm not saying to overextend, but I am saying there is nothing wrong with bringing the table, the food, the drinks, *and* the chairs. I mean, you do what you want when you poppin', right? Don't block your blessings and potential opportunities by allowing the voices of other people to influence your actions. How you're choosing to set yourself up for success is between you and the person looking back at you in the mirror.

As we embrace the spirit of "doing the most" and reject limitations, we unlock the power of being original and unique. That power of being original and unique is inherent in all of us. But the power we get by homing in on that uniqueness and owning it in every aspect of our being—whether that's personal, professional, spiritual, or however—is the process that requires self-mastery. We're all capable of opening doors, but how are you walking through them? Are you rushing through them so fast that you end up getting a cramp? Are you waltzing through them and admiring the architecture of the rooms? And, more importantly, are you opening them up wide enough for those who will come in after you? (More on this later.)

On the path of discovering my uniqueness, I also discovered the importance of self-validation. My first professional performance on the set of *Barbershop 2* was a thrilling experience, but also a challenging one. I was cast as Queen Latifah's smart-mouthed niece in the presence of Ice Cube, Cedric the Entertainer, and so many others at just nine years old. I was excited, nervous, and eager to prove myself. I wanted to show everyone that I had what it took to succeed in the entertainment industry. I was only on set for four days, but whenever I left, my mother—my biggest cheerleader—would grill me about my day, asking me tough questions that made me think critically about my performance.

"How'd it go?"

"It went really well!" I'd recount, step-by-step, all that had happened from the time we got to base camp up until the time we left.

"Did the director give you any notes?"

Notes? I was confused. I shook my head and she laughed at my expression. "That means you're doing so well he had nothing to say."

I beamed. I thought about how Kevin, the director, spoke to some of the other actors around me at the time. Sometimes his face would wrinkle with dissatisfaction; sometimes he would be nodding, impressed with the performance, from his director's chair. I never noticed that he didn't have anything to say to me until my mother pointed it out. Now that I knew that I wasn't doing anything wrong, I'd wear my pride like a shiny-ass badge. I couldn't help but feel like I'd eaten one of those level-up mushrooms in *Super Mario Bros*.

But life has a way of shattering illusions, and the next day I got a dose of reality. It's like the universe needed to remind me that I still had a lot to learn. Kevin started giving me tons of feedback, asking me to tone it down and then to amp it up. Then there was *Lean on your right*, *Don't block your light*, and *Make sure you hit your mark*. Roll my eyes at this part, not this part. Run back inside on this cue, not the other. There was so much mental choreography that I started to get anxious. My mother's words—*Did he give you any notes?*—were stuck on repeat in my mind, a mental marquee scrolling in every font imaginable, from Comic Sans to my old-school fave Curlz MT. Needless to say, I took his direction as a sign that I was doing something wrong. I stumbled over words and caught myself overthinking all the things that had been coming naturally to me in the first takes.

Looking back now, it's safe to say that when I ran off the set, I was experiencing one of my earliest anxiety attacks. I was completely overwhelmed with the stress of what Kevin wanted from me. I was desperate to meet Kevin's expectations, and in doing so, I had tied my own worth to his validation. I ran off the set after what felt like my umpteenth note for the day. Kevin found me in the back room and affirmed I was doing a really great job. I was doing so great that he would even let me keep my character's off-brand but very chic shoes.

So yes, there was a little bribery (and I loved, loved, loved those shoes until my feet outgrew them! Or did I lose them? Damn), but at that point I knew the only way forward meant wiping my tears and nailing the scene to the best of my abilities, even though I was embarrassed that they all saw me have that very childish moment. I knew it would've been even more embarrassing to myself had I not got up and tried again.

On the ride home, my mother and I finally got some alone time to unpack my emotional day on set. As I explained what had triggered me, her expression turned from guilt to redemptive, and she apologized sincerely. I felt relieved, knowing she hadn't realized the impact of her words. She gently clarified that while her previous comment might be true, directors often seek different performances, and feedback isn't about good or bad—it's about exploration. "It's part of the process," she said, her words soothing my concerns.

To know my mother's words didn't have to be received the way I received them, which was disempowering, felt like a glass of water after a seventy-five-mile run (talk about *relief!*). Because to not be addressed at all in a working environment is impossible, but to know you will and can take direction, course-correcting as best you can, is a little more empowering. Her awareness of her actions made me feel capable, and her objective conversations about what transpired helped me develop a valuable skill: depersonalizing and finding solutions. She'd analyze cause and effect, showing me that the issue is never me, but rather my thinking and approach. This skill became crucial on set, especially with directors, and in any collaborative environment. I learned to handle stressors by focusing on my best efforts, not perfection. Committing to trying my best always beats perfection.

I learned to separate my performance from my personal emotions by establishing a clear boundary: I am not my work, but I do my work. This distinction allowed me to buffer criticism between my work and the master of my work—the real me. To learn how to take myself out of the performance and, instead, observe what was needed to best benefit the whole production. This marked the beginning of my process with detaching myself from my own feelings, which came with a loss of innocence as I learned to be a professional around many adults. By doing so, I gained the ability to focus on the craft, navigate feedback with clarity, and grow as an artist.

But being a child actor meant I was trapped in a triple bind: striving to be the perfect child, the perfect student, and the perfect coworker. That pressure was creating crippling depression. The fear of embarrassing my parents or being labeled an ungrateful child star was a heavy weight on my small shoulders. (And, yes, I've got nice traps to show for it—a small consolation!) My rapid rise to fame terrified my parents, and being under that magnifying glass made mistakes feel impossible. I saw my peers and colleagues get torn apart in the public eye, and I was desperate to avoid the same fate. I felt like I was living in a fishbowl, which would've been fine if I was accompanied by Nemo and Dory, but NOPE, just me (yes, that's a small *Nope* reference because me and Emerald both slayed the spectacle in our lives, mine being fame and hers being an otherworldly alien that won't leave her neighborhood. Twinsies!). I yearned to be truly selfish out loud, to experience the normal struggles of adolescence—like getting into a girl fight over a stupid high school boy or debating my teacher in front of the class. I wanted to share my grievances on set, to simply be a kid, because that's a child's right. Just like on the set of *Barbershop 2* when I freaked out, I was just being a kid. But when I chose to be a performer, I accepted that the business was unforgiving—and whenever I had a moment of weakness, no one gave me the grace of being a child, not even myself. And as a little Black child, I knew that racism already threatened to steal my innocence, but the pressures of fame added another layer of complexity. It wasn't just the weight of being Black; it was the weight of being a Black child in the public eye, with no room for error or childhood mistakes because "everybody is counting on you." I felt like I was losing myself in the process of always trying to make everyone proud. Like I was being forced to grow up too quickly, without the chance to experience the carefree joy of childhood. And even though my life is unique to me, I have a feeling that many of you reading this who either share the same background or have a completely different background still know to some degree what it's like to have to grow up too fast. Maybe that's a part of it, or perhaps I see it that way because it's my projected experience. I'm not sure. I am sure I'm not sad about it, because it's pointless to dwell on it, but to know my experience is to know what it taught me on my journey of self-mastery. Let's keep chatting, we just gettin' started, beau!

By sixteen, my wardrobe was a carbon copy of 2009 office chic—blazers, blouses, and all. I was walking around like a real Doogie Howser or—if we're being technical—True Jackson, VP. For so much of my life, while I was performing other characters, I was also learning through them who I actually wanted to be. And when I left a role, I took a piece of them with me—a gesture, a phrase, a confidence. I discovered a liberating truth: who we are is not fixed, life is a fluid performance. What happens when we dare to step outside the story society has written for us? What happens when we improv? Alchemy. As I continue to perform, this time it's not through the lens of who people want me to be, but who I'm deciding to be. At the end of the day, aren't we all putting on a performance? The gag, is who's pulling your strings?

2
TUNING OUT THE NOISE

Josephine Baker represents everything that, in my own way, I'd like to be: a renaissance woman, a revolutionary performer, a multifaceted talent. The way she not only danced but expressed humor and awareness onstage in her banana skirt in the show *Danse Sauvage* remains a landmark moment in entertainment history. Her expression holds an intriguing blend of allure and quirkiness, as if she's perpetually in on a private joke. It's as if she's watching you watch her, aware of the effect she has on you and using it to her advantage. At the same time, there's also something sultry in her movements, a sense of passion and distinct style that I admire. With a subtle nod to her own power, she dances around expectations, maintaining an air of mastery that's both captivating and unnerving. This is the essence I strive to embody in my own performances—a delicate balance of vulnerability and control.

I'm always in awe of how Josephine Baker unapologetically

brought her beauty and Blackness center stage with unparalleled style. She fearlessly rocked diverse looks, from short finger waves to high ponytails with yaki hair, and stunned audiences with dramatic pieces across Europe. By doing so, she gave mainstream visibility to Black culture, paving the way for future generations. When I think about her tangible impact on globalizing Black art and culture, I'm inspired to follow in her footsteps. I believe in and want to represent these values, too, because I share her passion for celebrating our culture's beauty and significance.

Josephine Baker's legacy endures because she dared to challenge the status quo, defying the entrenched systems meant to limit her potential as a Black American woman. The barriers to entry for Black people and people of color in any industry are dense and it doesn't matter if it's Hollywood or Silicon Valley, but Baker's story shows that success is not solely defined by one's country of origin. By leaving the United States and achieving greatness elsewhere, she exemplified the power of seeking solutions outside the constraints of a discriminatory system. It's a testament to the idea that one's worth and potential are not bound by the limitations of where they're from. As I like to say: Who says America is the only place you can be "great"?

(See what I did there? Huge sigh.)

What I'm saying is, Josephine Baker proved that you can create a path where none exists. And her leaving didn't mean she was running away and just leaving it all behind. During the civil rights movement, she returned to the United States and played a significant role in shedding light on the very issues that had driven her away. Josephine Baker wouldn't be the icon we revere today if she hadn't bet on herself and ventured beyond the constraints of America. How much more insular would our culture be if she hadn't crossed those borders to live an extraordinary life, defying the limitations of her time?

Society loves to tell us what's of value, but the true fear is not in taking the bait and believing you're worthless; it's actually in believing that you are worthy, important, and capable. Because once you know this, you have to *be* that in action. This is something I learned from artists like Josephine Baker, who taught me to go where you are loved, not merely tolerated, and push up against that red tape. I see this reflected in performers like Eartha Kitt, Prince, and many more. They understood that being an entertainer can be a visceral expression of our activism. While some may view our work as all glamour and glitz, for many of us, it's deeply intertwined with purpose. Just like with anybody else who is blessed to do a version of what they love every day, that gratitude can easily turn into servitude. When you're a deeply dedicated artist, the audience wants you to keep playing your role. You might play until your toes bleed, and even then the show must go on—because your purpose has become intertwined with the performance. The lines between your art and your identity begin to blur, and the movement you're a part of becomes a living, breathing entity that propels you forward. You become a vessel for the message, and the message becomes the driving force. In this dynamic, it's easy to lose sight of where the performance ends and your life begins.

This is why it's crucial to separate your purpose from your right to be. Meaning, you deserve to exist and be yourself regardless of how or when you fulfill your purpose. We often look to external measures to gauge our progress and confirm we're on the right track—whether it's an accolade or simply a pat on the back. But the truth is our purpose can't be measured by external validation alone. It's easy to get caught up in seeking external confirmation, but faith must come into play.

Our purpose doesn't have a time frame; it can be fulfilled in an instant or unfold over time. None of us know when we'll find our thing, and that's okay. The key is to look inward first, trusting that our internal guidance will lead us forward, even when external validation is scarce.

Staying focused on you, with how you feel being your greatest gauge, is the only way to reach your fullest potential. I'm grateful for the people in my life who helped me learn to separate my personal value from my professional accomplishments. But let's be real, it's easy to get sucked into the "I'm going to save the world" vortex—I mean, who doesn't want to be a superhero, right? (Marvel, CALL ME!) However, that mindset is not only delusional but also exhausting. As Mother Teresa wisely said, "We can't do great things, only small things with great love." So, I just aim for making a difference in my own small, loving way—no cape required! (Until Marvel calls me, of course.)

When I first entered the entertainment industry, I had limited professional stage experience beyond school and church plays. The way my parents talked about Broadway intimidated me, and I doubted my chances of landing a role. However, when I finally made it to Broadway, it was incredibly rewarding—the best experience of my life at that point. It felt like my birthright, and I reveled in the instant gratification of connecting with the audience in real time. Our energies intertwining as I brought Cinderella's story to life through acting, singing, and dancing. In that moment, my parents' training made sense; they had prepared me to be a versatile performer. Onstage, I felt unstoppable and finally understood as a film girl that my heart was from the theater.

The feeling is no different from finding your niche in an industry you love. When you declare your passion for saving lives and then realize you want to be a doctor, only to later discover your true calling as an orthopedic or ob-gyn specialist—that's powerful. Similarly, my journey evolved from wanting to evoke emotions, to singing in church, to embracing the trifecta of music, dance, and acting. But what I didn't realize until I experienced theater was that I was always a dramatic theater kid at heart—I just didn't know it yet. All the extra flair and dramatics I brought to my work were validated in that moment. I felt proud to be a "theater type" and understood that it was okay to bring that level of passion and expression to everything I do. Broadway solidified this for me, and now I'm unafraid to lean into my theatrical nature, knowing it's a strength that sets me apart.

The great thing about Broadway is that they teach you to be more than ready for the stage. You practice again and again. Even when you feel like you're about to pass out from exhaustion or get spooked by nerves, your mind defaults to the countless hours of practice—whether that is the one-two step dance sequence or the classic "A Lovely Night." After they rehearse you, and rehearse you some more, and then rehearse you a million times over, it becomes second nature for you to slip right into what you know, what you practiced. Thank God for muscle memory built from a million repetitions!

On that first opening night, I was shaking from the adrenaline rush and my hands get really sweaty when I'm nervous, not to mention all the gas. Ahh! "WHAT IF I FORGET EVERYTHING?" I texted my family in a panic. Yet I knew exactly what to do. Looking back on the grueling schedule—daily shows, double matinees, and only Sundays off—plus the intense rehearsals, physical training, and strict vocal regimen, I realized that discipline trumps talent. The whole experience was a testament to the power of discipline, which became my guiding principle: with discipline, anything is possible. I recall a particularly chaotic quick-change moment when I had to transform from head to toe in a heartbeat. Amid the mess and frazzle, I had to mentally prepare to step back into the spotlight, leaving the chaos behind the curtains.

I remember asking the director, "How the hell am I going to do that?" while thinking to myself, *They done fucked up and hired the wrong person*. Singing and dancing wouldn't be enough; I needed to master the logistical demands of the role! As I made space for self-doubt, the show's expectations became truly concerning. The stage manager paid me no mind. In fact, he carried the confidence that I would soon find in my footing. "You'll get there," he said. And he was so relaxed in this truth that I almost believed it. I embraced that pseudo confidence, recognizing that my self-doubt was invading the sacred space where I felt most creative: onstage. I began to rewire my inner dialogue, whispering his reassuring phrase to myself: *You'll get there. You'll get there.* By granting myself the permission and space to figure things out, I was focused enough on the road to finally arrive at the destination. And before I knew it, I was navigating quick-change sequences with ease in under a minute. The transformation was remarkable, and I had given myself the grace to get there.

I think the phrase "trust the process" can sometimes seem like it's overused, but it's the most relevant piece of advice when backed by accountability and action. It was about trusting the process and its progress, while taking time to be patient with myself. And to have discipline in anything, you must be patient, because it's not the act of being perfect that gets you there, but rather the act of putting in the time and practice, trusting that you will. Just as I did during those intense rehearsals, I knew I wouldn't get it immediately, but I was absolutely certain I would get it eventually.

At the same time, let's not forget that this *was* my Broadway debut. The headlines didn't shy away from the historic nature of my lead role as the first Black Cinderella on Broadway. Nor did I—my mother and I were beaming with pride, especially since I grew up admiring Brandy, the first Black Cinderella ever! I felt thrilled to walk in her footsteps, but that also meant shouldering many more expectations. Some people took the excitement surrounding my historic role as an opportunity to point out the ongoing struggles with diversity and representation in theater. As if entertainers like Louis Armstrong, Ma Rainey, or Nina Simone didn't also bring attention to what it meant to be a Black artist in front of a live audience during their reigns on stages throughout the country. All things can be true: we can celebrate the amazing Black legends who have graced Broadway's stage, we can celebrate me for being the first Black Cinderella on Broadway, and we can still push for more diversity. Additionally, the entire production was mostly getting a lot of excitement, but this also influenced my desire to be my best leading up to opening night.

I decided to choose and maintain peace. And like many of my peers, I'm not one to go out seeking reviews, especially in spaces that have been historically cruel and overly critical of Black art no matter what the form. We see it today in everything from music to filmmaking. ("16 Carriages!") I tune out the noise because I do believe that art is subjective. If I feel good about my performance, and my director feels good about my performance, and the audience was entertained, then I've done the best that I could. Oh, and that's not to say that people pay for these reviews... but I regard reviews similarly to how I view awards. Where they have value is where you put value on them. And this may be a hot take, but I don't put tons of value in these institutions. I put value on the people I'm working with: my cast members, the director, the production, the stage crew—and their experiences. And if they're crazy, then f*** them, too. (I kid, I kid . . .) I'll run to my mother about how she felt about my performance before I consult a pressroom. Trust me, I know Sharon, and she won't hold any punches.

My favorite movies come from the '90s and early 2000s. I'm talking Black Hollywood (if they had an ingenious name like "the Brat Pack," I wonder what it'd be?). I'm talking Taye Diggs, Larenz Tate, Omar Epps, Morris Chestnut, Nia Long, Sanaa Lathan, Vivica A. Fox, Gabrielle Union, and so on. Movies like *The Wood*. I'm talking *Love & Basketball*. I'm talking *Deliver Us from Eva*, *The Best Man*, and *Soul Food*. There are several things I would consider neglecting just to watch Taye Diggs and Sanaa Lathan cozy up in *Brown Sugar*.

I love a lot of the work that Rick Famuyiwa has done. But movies like these would get an audience score that didn't reflect how I experienced them, which typically meant feeling seen, observing balanced and nuanced cultural representation, and rolling on the floor, dying of laughter. These movies were simply good storytelling across the board. I remember when *Mea Culpa* came out and it was getting a lot of buzz and press everywhere. Obviously, my girl Kelly Rowland was starring in it, which was amazing because she doesn't grace us with her presence often. Then Trevante Rhodes, because, of course, who doesn't love talented eye candy? The cinematography was expensive, the chemistry between the leads was electric, to say the least, and Netflix was clearly invested in Tyler Perry's vision. But the reviews that came out were unnecessarily brutal in my opinion, not only from the press but also from the Black community, or Black Twitter, I should say. Both of which, I think, are reflective of what I mentioned above, in similar but different ways: There is not understanding Black culture enough to appreciate the nuances that exist unbeknownst to you (films like

The Wood). Then there is not critiquing art through the lens of your opinion but by its appropriate genre (Tyler). Building on that point: Black art often has an unnecessarily critical light shined on it. Where it puts this unrealistic pressure on Black creatives to always make some huge community reflective project when sometimes people just want to entertain you and help you escape. This is how the Black exploitation era of films was prematurely dismissed and so many Black-owned production companies lost their business after those movies saved Hollywood, judged improperly for simply their style and popularity. It's only decades later when documentaries have been made to shine a light on that time and give those movies their due respect for what they innovated. Including Quentin Tarantino paying homage with *Pulp Fiction* and me in my movie *Alice*. I do the best I can at resisting the hyperawareness of the white gaze and our marginalization so I can respect and appreciate how others choose to express their experiences in their art. I think Tyler Perry has a unique style and it's what has made him, him. It's very theatrical, fantastical, and ridiculous (in a fun way to me), often serving to emphasize a moral lesson through heightened storytelling. There is no wrong or right in creating. Creating is creating, and his vision is consistent, which means it's on purpose and not by mistake. That means he has cemented his style, and that's not easy. Doesn't mean you have to like it, but I guess I do want to highlight this unbelievable pressure Black artists continue to face. That stems from this desire to be seen on the "main stage" that often lacks cultural understanding and, in turn, makes us hypercritical of the ones who do break through that ceiling. People say they want diversity within our community, but when it's not what they like, it has to cease to exist. That's the problem that respectability politics places on Black creativity. Whether you like it or not, in our fight for diversity, these films have a right to exist and be criticized with respect to their culture and genre. You don't compare Steven Spielberg and Quentin Tarantino, so why compare Tyler Perry to Spike Lee? Oh, simply because they're Black... got it. Diversity should exist in our genres and in our reviews. Until then, I don't care. This was my same issue with *Get Out*: it wasn't a comedy. Or is Black trauma a joke? Did it brilliantly use satirical elements to highlight the bone-chilling drama of being the only Black person in any space? YES! This highlights the lack of evolution in Hollywood when it comes to some of their institutions. They have not caught up to how culture and genre are evolving. That particularly pisses me off when it comes to creatives like Jordan because he's a genre bender in a way that truly inspires me to be limitless as a storyteller.

And I'm not saying there aren't people who have done the work of being fair in their reviews, just that the history of viewership and art and how it's perceived when artists are taking risks and dabbling in something different is always up for critique.

And... exhale. That was one way I chose to maintain my peace while on Broadway. On the other end, I found myself relying on the comments and reposts on social media because that's where my actual audience lived. The people commenting and responding to me were those who understood not only my work but me as a talent, so they were basing their reviews off me. They were not basing their reviews off what's out there; it's not based in comparison to others. Sometimes it can be, but those are usually not really your fans. It is based on the comparison of your earlier work to your most recent work. Still, in order to do what I do from the place I do it from, I have to take even that with a grain of salt.

In our business, I feel like there's a collective understanding that reviews can impact how people feel about you at that moment, but they don't impact how you see yourself if you don't allow them to. And so, yeah, I understand why we place value on these markers of external validation, and I get the concept of it, but most times I actively choose not to participate. And I don't know, maybe that's how my mom raised me, to remain afloat.

Or let me break it down further. You know what it's like? It's the equivalent of going to work and getting an incredible performance review. Then, a week later, a new manager comes to your desk and says, "I actually didn't think you were good." This person may be someone with expertise in your field but, regardless, they wouldn't fully understand the places you have to get to (mentally) or have the wherewithal about what it takes to do what you did to be where you are currently in the company. So all those people you worked with, they loved it, they love you, and they thought you were great, and you did exactly what they asked you to do. Now you have a new person saying "I don't really like it" and judging your work by factors that weren't even present before they came. How does that really add up? Who would I be if I absorbed every piece of media when, ultimately, my primary concern is if I did my job? Every new manager ain't good and every new manager don't last. Y'all know.

It's dangerous to have outside voices in the space where you're the most creative version of yourself. And I'll admit that it's a really tough but necessary skill to have. Or else, all your life, you'll be looking to the validation of others who may not even have your goal in mind—and where's your power in that? I place value in spaces I know I will be valued and where my goals are aligned. That's a big part of it, because what's good to me ain't good to you and the meaning of success to me isn't success to you, so how can I let you be the judge?

And so, if I know I did the job with my utmost effort and

professionalism, then take it up with management, Sweets. Because I did the job I was asked to do.

To work in the industry means that the boundaries of work are blurred, and so is our relationship to the work. It's understandable when collaborations blossom into romantic relationships over months of intense shooting schedules and shared creative passions. There are intimate moments during long days, longer hours, and a lot of talking outside the sounds of the slate. Then there are people working in a whisper network around you, commenting on how "cute" the two of you look together and how you would make the "perfect couple." And think about it, the fandom around celebrities not only moves the needle forward on the movie just filmed, but also on each of them as individuals. Now more people are invested in what projects are in the pipeline and if your current partner will be there to support you. Or if in your next project the lead is more attractive than the last and speculations about this new dynamic on set. Put two conventionally attractive leads together, have them be spotted by paparazzi in a few places, and then in a year or two they may break up. Rinse and repeat.

The thing that disappoints me is when these conversations become more about the relationship than the work. The stories about relationships begin to eclipse the months or weeks spent on set. It's a different beast now, with dedicated social media pages solely for updates on couples with pictures from the past and with news sites writing articles about "Voldemort's Dating History: From Harry's Mom to Snape" or "A Timeline of Leonardo da Vinci's Complete Dating History." It's invasive at the very least, but the idea of getting to the bag or doing the work and not complaining is so rooted in our society and can slowly blur out, especially for a child, what is normal and what isn't. To have reminders of your relationship while you're mindlessly scrolling down your own For You page is low-key triggering. And while a trip down memory lane can be nostalgic and fun, no one truly knows what's on the other side of a photographed image. I was so uninterested in dating coworkers, but I still understood that there was a performance aspect that the two people involved would mutually agree upon, and it was one I could appreciate.

I'll admit I had a handful of awkward age-gap scenarios. *Jump In!* was seventeen years ago, and as much as I love my brother Corbin Bleu, I remember thinking of him exactly like that—as a brother. Thankfully, our fans of the movie didn't make it into more than what it was because, as a twelve-year-old, the last thing I wanted was an article about a tween power couple—which everyone was obsessed with at the time. Before we shared our on-screen kiss, I remember my agent at the time saying, "It's going to be fine. It happens all the time and it's not really *your* real first kiss, it's a movie character's first kiss." Then she went ahead and shared a story about one of her former clients, someone I admire actually, who had to share an on-screen kiss with a nearly fifty-year-old man as a minor. She laughed. I cringed. I always wondered if she could sense how that revelation didn't make me feel any better.

On a set a few years later, I felt absolutely humiliated after shooting a scene where things were getting a little risqué between my character and another who was played by someone a decade older than me. I wasn't as experienced in my personal life, and when the director yelled "Action!" I did the best I could in the scene. My costar was being pretty insensitive about it with the director. He thought I was being unprofessional, and looking back I feel like he probably was shy as well and was taking my behavior personally, but I genuinely was just an inexperienced, awkward teen. Having a passionate make-out session with a person I actually liked was still a new thing! This time, I didn't turn to my agent or confide in anyone about how I was feeling. I just walked to the bathroom and had myself a little cry.

This was part of the job. To make the things that I'd sometimes never experienced believable to an audience on the other side of the screen, and my own teammate was making me feel inadequate. I kept performing through this discomfort, thinking I'd done a good job hiding my vulnerabilities. Until another costar, Dolly Parton, ended up providing more comfort to me as we moved on to the next scene. When I came out of the bathroom, it's like she saw right through me and whispered in her lil southern twang, "I'll kiss those pretty ole lips." In that moment I felt so seen, like only Dolly Parton could compliment you like that and make you feel both beautiful again and heard. And she probably doesn't even remember saying that, but it meant a lot to me.

The work I'd done making sure to not take things so personally from years prior had been holding up well, but there were always moments when the cracks showed. My attitude faltered. It happens, and it's okay. Similar to how I handled myself years earlier on the set of *Barbershop 2*, I dusted myself off and tried again. There will always be setbacks. I think that's the funniest thing: When we learn lessons, we think that means that nothing like that will ever happen again. That we experienced it once and we'll never have to again. I don't think life is like that; I think it's actually about experiencing many different versions of the same triggers and it's your bounce-back rate that proves sufficiency. There will always be tests, but the point is to go from a C to a B to an A-plus.

3

THE FREEDOM TO SAY NO

My desire to shift gears in my career came out of both inspiration and necessity. There was a time when nobody was booking me for any jobs (the audacity!). I was embarrassed, tired, and worried about disappointing my family because I knew they had become reliant upon me financially. The stress of knowing that they had sacrificed so much of their time, money, and life into this brand—this *Keke Palmer machine*—made me very driven but also very stressed. I wouldn't and couldn't allow myself to fail because of them. At the same time, the fame that I had acquired scared my parents so much and they so deeply feared people were using my success as a way to disempower them. So I developed this sense of impostor syndrome where I could no longer amount my success to who *I* was, and any acknowledgment in the beauty of who I am was apparently only because I was successful, as opposed to the reality that I am successful because I am this person. The way my parents would counteract both their fear of the dynamic shift and of me being taken advantage of was to emphasize that the way people treated me was solely based on what they could gain from me. While both things can be true at once, fame and success can bring on hangers-on, but I can also be a genuinely lovable person. After a while, when people told me I was amazing, I truly could not believe or trust that they were telling the truth. It's hard when you believe your value is attached to what you do and the amount of money you make.

This was especially difficult when I felt I could no longer afford a certain lifestyle. I'm not talking buying bags and shoes; I mean the lifestyle of helping to support those I cared for. My family moved back to Chicago—because I could no longer afford to keep them and myself in LA—while I went to work in Atlanta. My anxieties were not only present in my mind, but also in my body. I would have panic attacks regularly but wouldn't share them out of shame for making my parents feel guilty. My periods were so irregular, they would disappear for months. I thought it was easier to suffer in silence, alone, and would often find solace journaling. I had to work hard to understand and let go of the idea that other people were my responsibility, which I ironically found freedom in after actually becoming responsible for a small child (more on that later). I was also on a critical mission: I needed to find the joy in performing again.

I'd aged out of my popularity group and had to rebuild my brand in a new generation. And our generation had evolved into social media. The ability to connect directly to my audience and create the things I wanted to create for them (*without* going through gatekeepers) meant I had an opportunity to actually show what I had to give and be all that I wanted to be. Also, there were simply so many spaces that people like me and my peers weren't allowed to be in yet.

And just because you're auditioning doesn't mean they're watching the tape. There's no joy in spending hours in front of a video camera for potential employers who may or may not even review what you spent so much time putting together. It's quite disheartening. Still, I would record my audition tapes reciting lines from a script, but there was this harsh, blaring undertone that made me cringe. It's like I was jumping up and down, saying, "Look at me! Look at me! I need this! Don't you like me? Don't you?"

That initial burnout from auditioning so much really did a number on me. It was exhausting. Yet, I knew *that* was the system and inside my frustration was a quality of surrendering to the reality that I wasn't going to be able to change the system itself, but I could change the way I operated in it. I started studying, watching, and seeing how people were using social media in this new digital age. I realized if I really wanted to stay in this, I had to invest in myself and be okay with the fact that it was going to be a financial sacrifice that I was going to have to make. A gamble, so to speak, betting on me! At the same time, I was excited about the opportunity to share what made me unique, in a way that I could not when trying to fit into the shape of a traditional system. Since a young age, through the medium of performance art, I was always told I had a preternatural ability to bring people together. You know when you're in a movie theater watching a film with random people you don't know? Well, the performers playing those roles brought you all together. It's the same thing with a concert, an art gallery, or watching a president speak at their inauguration. Beyond drawing a crowd via my performing a particular piece, even when I would speak at schools, I knew that I *spoke* in a way that would make older people listen and in a way that my generation could relate to. I was also embracing and accepting the challenge at large. I was excited for this change as a child artist who'd evolved into this adult life with an incredible fan base. I had to keep asking myself: What's the new story I'm telling? And how do I get people to continue tuning in?

When I worked with Nickelodeon and Disney, I was attentive as hell. I paid attention to everything like never before. They were basically paying for people to teach me how to be a 360 entertainer. Who was I to *not* be taking notes? And thank God for my mother; she was someone who really told me to focus when I had the opportunity to break into those early spaces. Back then I didn't realize I was learning how to build the foundation for what would be the current Keke Palmer brand you see today.

The other day, I did a whole content shoot brought to you by what I call the School of Disney. It was tough and it was a lot of work, but I filmed five different characters, did twelve different setups of different content pieces that I got to roll out on my own network on Instagram, KeyTV, Facebook, Snapchat, and TikTok. I've been able to take the tools I've acquired to run my own business, the business of Keke. But it took a lot of discipline and commitment.

I started becoming an artist in a way that felt fun and natural to me. It was also liberating because I was calling the shots, and it was freeing that nobody could tell me they did or didn't like it. And when they did give criticism, if it was constructive in a way that made me want to elevate my content for the people I wanted to communicate with the most, I would embrace it. At the end of the day, it was my relationship with my audience that I focused on building. And I was committed.

One time I was working on a show with a grueling schedule, but it didn't matter to me because I absolutely admired the creator, Ryan Murphy. I wasn't a main character in the first season, though I still had a good amount of airtime. Pretty soon my role expanded, which meant in the second season I was more involved—which, again, was so incredible.

On any set, your schedule is subject to be in flux. That's the gig you sign up for! However, I was already years deep into being a multihyphenate entertainer. The schedule for the show was always changing and it was really difficult to figure out what days I would or wouldn't have off. Sometimes the scripts wouldn't even be written, which isn't that common, so they couldn't schedule in advance. I was working on music and building my digital brand all at the same time. My business and brand were flourishing because of my continued perseverance. On set, when they gave me specific days off, I would build my other investments around these blocks. But one day, when it came time for me to leave, they decided to go back on what they said. I was both confused and furious. In that moment I knew I would lose a lot of money if I didn't leave the set right then. Not only that, but I also knew that I was giving that job everything they asked of me, and they had promised me something that was important to me: time. Something they didn't care about even though I was putting them above everything. I gave that show all my time like any one of us does any job and I just asked for days that they agreed to in order to give me some time to invest in myself.

It wasn't like they hadn't agreed; they just didn't seem to care. But I did, which was enough for me. I knew I could get fined, but I left the set anyway.

At the end of it all, they (not so surprisingly) finished the episode without my physical presence by using my stand-in. Not only was this not a *huge* issue, but our continuity person was the actual director that week, which meant she was the perfect person to shoot the scenes with me while I was absent. She knew the angles to use to make it seem as if I was present on camera. Honestly, she got to shine, so I love that for her. But my leaving didn't mean I came out unscathed. I had to deal with the consequences of standing my ground. Ryan was really angry with me. He ripped into me, and I took it, because I did something unprofessional, which is quite unlike me. I apologized. I told him that I was building my brand and that I respected the show, but the days I was promised were the days I was promised. While I was unprofessional, so were they. And in my humble independent contractor opinion, I reserved the right to respond to them the way they had responded to me: by accepting the consequences.

I would've lost money and pieces of my integrity had I not left the set. I'm still not sure Ryan cared, or got it, and that's okay because he was just centering his business, which isn't a problem to me. But what I do know is even if he didn't care, and even if I never work with him again, he knows that I, too, see myself as a business. Not just someone in need of employment but someone who knows their value, respectfully. Bottom line, I bet on myself every day and I've never looked back. I know I'm a good collaborator, but I'm also a fair collaborator. All I was asking for was some fairness. I was willing to risk my job. To die on the hill of me being worth the respect I was asking for. And maybe if it had been the first season, I might have felt differently, but at that time I weighed the options of what I was gaining and what I would be losing. I looked at the bigger picture for what I wanted to do and based my decision off that. I think an important callout when deciding to take risks is seeing how they tie into your ultimate goal, which only you know. I haven't worked for him since, but I damn sure haven't stopped working and have continually aligned with the things that fit the career *I* see for myself. And there are no hard feelings; I'm still a fan of his.

The freedom to say no is so big, but it really does take time and confidence to get there. It took a long time for me to get to this level of liberation. All I'm saying is, you never know what will happen if you speak up, or if you don't. So don't underestimate the power of your voice.

There's this scene in the 1995 rom-com film *Waiting to Exhale* that I think about often. And no, I'm not talking about Bernadine (played by the one and only Angela Bassett) and her incredible monologue that ends with her setting her cheating husband's clothes on fire in his car, on their driveway, and strutting away like the Boss-Ass Bitch she is. "732, the number of times that we made love!" (I digress, but this really is a top-tier moment in film history.)

In the particular scene that I'm referencing, Savannah (played by Whitney Houston) has this long, drawn-out exhale while having sex with a married man. She could be releasing that orgasm—which, to be clear, I love that for her—but she also ends up leaving him later on in the film. To me it's clear that she most likely knew that when she was having sex with him, she wasn't doing it for him. She was doing it for herself and doing that until it no longer worked for her.

Throughout the movie, I love how all these women walk along different paths to reach that final scene where their arms are raised and they're able to toast to a new year without a care in the world. I personally feel that as women, we are all waiting to exhale. This analogy didn't make much sense to me as a youth, but I had a revelation about it in my new, thirty-year-aged wisdom when I realized maybe it means doing something different than you normally would. We are often doing this subconsciously—kind of what I talked about before, things that are habits. That we were born into doing and being, as opposed to making a choice. A lot of times acting in ways that go against our nature, like holding our breath.

For me, the act of exhaling is the act of being selfish. And not in the way that they make you think about this word and hate it, but *selfish* in the neutral sense. The kind of selfish that's simply autonomous. It doesn't mean you're being dishonest or mean or inconsiderate. It just means you're centering your needs and not wavering them where you cannot exist as your true self.

There's this idea that certain women are expected to perform certain roles in society, that being passive or deferential to men is a way forward. For clarity, I disagree. I disagree with the idea that, as women, it's weak to be passive or that there is no space for respect for the opposite sex. And I disagree with this notion that as a woman there is no scenario or situation where it is constructive or okay to *not* be. There are so many people I admire, like Whoopi Goldberg and Bette Midler, who've made a career of going against this notion. Not going out of their way to be opposing, but living in their authenticity, which simply opposes what we as women are often told we should be, naturally. Even Beyoncé stands for everything that opposes misogyny. She plays her aesthetic against itself by presenting as a southern belle while speaking on female dominance, personal power, and standing in *your* truth. What's wrong with femininity being powerful?

Feminism, to me, doesn't exist in a vacuum. In fact, at its core, feminism truly is about the right to be an individual. A lot of people think feminism is the response to misogyny, but that's misandry. Feminism only exists because of the terror misogyny elicits upon women and men. If women were allowed to be more empowered, both legally and literally as well as metaphorically and societally, so many more men would be as well. These rigid gender rules hinder everyone involved, and another movie moment I look to is Greta Gerwig's *Barbie*.

Barbie did a good job exploring how the patriarchy is the death of individualism and feminism is a way to find our way back. Ken, Ryan Gosling's character, spoke to that in so many moments, especially when it came to his manhood being defined by what he owned and what kind of woman he had. His desire to validate his manhood through all these things that the patriarchy put on him by default made him a misogynist and confused him on his sense of value. When Barbie discovers herself, it further confuses Ken, simply because the patriarchy needs both to agree in order for it to exist.

From the fall of Barbie World to the introduction of Barbie into our world, I found myself really invested in how the movie displayed this aspect of individualism so well. When any one of us decides to be an individual and base our value on what we think is important, we shake the entire system and how it's meant to control our sense of self.

4

FREAK THE SYSTEMS AT LARGE

The true currency is time and how you spend it. As long as you're still standing, your time is never up. You are the truest asset in any space you walk in and what you have to offer in your essence. And, trust me, we both know you have a lot to offer. Even if you're working for someone else, you should still be negotiating with yourself about what you think is worth your time and what isn't. What are you willing to let go of and what aren't you? All these questions should appear alongside you while you're walking towards your purpose, this thing that brings you joy and light. Something that you can shout to the moon about being proud of. And whether that's supporting your side hustle of selling incredible pastries with a dream of opening your own bakery or helping kids in after-school programs in order to find your way in the front of a classroom, every step you take should contribute in some way to those dreams.

I really do believe that we're priceless people. Every human being made under God. So, to me, the concept of going into a job, or any career, thinking that somebody is going to pay you your *worth*, I don't know that that's possible. I say that with not one jaded bone in my body but as an earth sign, if I may bring the zodiac into it, I have to be a realist. If the business in which we work as human beings and the value we have as human beings are to be equated in any regard, you're always going to be disappointed. Nobody in the world is ever going to be paid their true worth. There's not enough money that they can give you that will actually equate to what your actual worth is. Everything in a corporation is about business, and business is simply about money. It's not yourself that you are leveraging, because that would make it personal, and for me it just simply cannot be. It's the amount of business you can bring in. And when you reframe time as the biggest and most rewarding currency you have, the question becomes: How can you use it to your benefit?

Maximizing your time plays an important part when working with corporations, and sometimes looking at them as a trade school can be more useful than looking at them as a job or career. Because even if you feel you are not being paid enough, you can think about the transferable skills and how the job offers you something you can learn. Think of how you can put this skill on your résumé. Think about it as trying to leverage what you are learning at the company. A big part of freeing myself from the idea of a corporate overlord is looking at what I'm learning and the skill the job allows me to acquire as a stepping stone, so that I always feel like I'm going forward and not standing still. Maintaining excitement in one's personal goals is important, as it's very easy to confuse your goals with a corporation's goals and before you know it, you could be another rat in their race.

And understanding your own value, what you want to do, and how your time reflects that allows you to move with intention, which, for me, is quite empowering. It's about objectivity. And one thing about time, as we know, is that it's something we can't get back.

There's a process to creating a system that works for you. The first step is being honest with yourself. For me, I knew I wanted to continue entertaining, but not forever—especially not at this level. As I said before, although I love performing, I love making people feel things more than anything and I love that sense of community I was able to tap into *through* performing. As my understanding of myself evolved, so did my goals. I knew I wanted to create something that would allow me to be a conduit for others. To be able to transfer the skills I learned throughout my years of entertainment and business experience and build a platform for others to use as a launchpad in their pursuit of entrepreneurship. The community that exists within myself as I write this book and within the readers who are reading it. (Hey, y'all!) There was obviously a long process to getting there both mentally and financially. It meant taking the money I was getting from my main job—my main gig as an actor—and putting it into the things that were important to me with the hope and desire that they might turn into other opportunities. And the journey isn't linear at all. In fact, you'll run into dead ends, then double back. You'll bust a U-turn, and potentially run into several nasty potholes in the process. Here I am, a living testament, almost twenty-three years into cultivating my own brand, saying, "I did it!" And you can do it, too.

The second step is understanding that there's a certain level of discipline and accountability that goes into making this work serve you. It's not always about how good you are at the actual job; it's also about how you show up to the job as well. Are you on time? Do you have a good attitude? Are you efficient? Are you flexible? Are you calm and collected under fire? Do you represent yourself well? Are you a good communicator? These are the things that talented people sometimes don't think matter. Honestly, you can double your rate in any field if you create an enjoyable experience for the client. And you can lower your rate when people don't like the experience of working with you, no matter the outcome of the actual task. I'm talented, but I'm not arrogant enough to believe that there aren't many talented people. However, not every talented person is a professional, and people pay for professionalism.

The third step is about awareness. Be aware of what you're up against, what the *climate* is, and then figure out how to make yourself work within it. Or, moreover, how to make yourself stand out doing what only *you* can do. This is what was really working for me. I leaned into every tool I had, until that tool became a real service provider. Now I'm not just working for them; they're working *with me* because they need collaborators like me who have a vision. My partners have a platform that they need people to engage with. They need people like me to be on the platform because not only does it give them content, but it also brings them viewership that's reserved for me via my fan base. No one is going to tell you *how* to empower yourself, but I want to tell people how to empower themselves with the truth. Because if you don't know how the system works, you can't make it work for you.

I think about how Kevin Hart is someone I look up to who came into the game and showed us how to freak the systems at large. I don't know the specifics of his entire journey, but I do know that he leveraged his social media and became a marketing maven where now these companies pay him to digitally market movies that he's already starring in. He now knows how to put together and produce his own digital content so he can leverage brand relationships. Like, my man has twelve different careers in one and he often spreads that knowledge. Not because he thinks he's so smart but because he took the time to understand the business and knows that way can empower others, too. Especially in a corporate America that can make any one of us, no matter the field, feel like we are just pawns in someone else's game.

Sometimes I do fear that we get in our own way. There are several times when I know that I've gotten in my own way because I've allowed fear or overthinking or hypothetical, nonsensical scenarios to plague my mind. We're humans, of course we internalize the wrong things a bit too much at times. It doesn't really serve you to constantly say, "Well if I had gone to private school" or "If I had grown up in this area and my mama hadn't permed my hair" or "If only I'd grown up vegan." (Okay, that last one is personal to me because damn it's hard to switch gears later in life.)

But what I'm saying is, the what-ifs are not important and can never be true. Because if you think about the person who has the ingredients that bake a sweet life, if you think that they're not having any issues because they have x, y, or z, then you're out of your damn mind! They may not have your issues, but they are gonna have issues. There is no life that is absolutely free of issues! There may be privilege, but every life has challenges and we were all built to withstand our own.

The truth is there are so many external factors in constant movement that you'll never really know why a lot of things are happening, why certain projects get off the ground or not. Sometimes it's really about divine timing. I had to remember that what is for you will be for you. When I was nine years old, I got my golden ticket to California to be part of *American Juniors*, which was Fremantle's kids' version of *American Idol*. I was so excited about the opportunity that I thought fame would be inevitable soon after.

But then I got cut from the pilot—along with child actors like Lucy Hale and Jordin Sparks—and I was really disappointed. At the time, it sucked. But, in hindsight, I'm so grateful that it didn't work out because I didn't get wrapped up in some of the early iterations of a 360 deal, which is basically a deal that encompasses everything and it's specific to music. The label, at this point, has their hand in every pocket you can make, from merch to clothing deals to any outside brand deals. And by the time I worked with Fremantle again, I was in a better place in my career and had enough going for me that I became the host of one of their oldest IPs when they decided to reboot *Password*. Had I worked with them from the start and become a contestant on *American Juniors*, I would've gotten tied up for years, unable to work with anyone else. That means no Atlantic record deal, no Disney Channel pilot, and no *The Wool Cap*. Three opportunities that are important factors in the foundation of my brand.

It's important you experience and do stuff that excites you, and that offers you the opportunity, without relying on the outcome. It's equally important in my opinion that sometimes you don't have the opportunity, because that informs your experience, too. Without that flexibility in thought, I think a lot of people can be stopped from being happy or from being appreciative, really. I've learned that having a sense of gratitude is a great source of power. To have faith that no matter how things go in your life, they're going the right direction for you. Mainly because we will never know the opposite. Genuinely, how can you know your life would've been better if you did this or that? You can't, therefore I choose to believe it wouldn't be. That belief keeps me in the present. When you believe that what did or didn't happen doesn't matter, what does does.

5
PUBLIC SERVICE ANNOUNCEMENT

The Virgo in me knows I don't want my personal life to overshadow the mission of my work. In fact, I know that my personal life will never compare to the magnitude of my life's work. And this isn't to say my private matters are small, because they're not, but I am aware that who I am as a person will never be as idealistic as my ideas, or what I create. My personal and professional lives will always remain two separate things and this, to me, was one of the hardest things to communicate to people who love me. And it was also hard to not engage with the public on that.

But now I'm gonna get a little personal. Just a little.

I was never in many public-facing relationships. One reason being my mother always made me afraid. She always told me I was a young woman on a mission and not to let a man come in and overshadow that mission. It sounds like my mom is a man-hater, but she's obsessed with my dad and gives "my man my man my man" energy, but I digress. As I grew into my own thoughts, I had the feeling that my relationships were something I would want to keep private. However, that can pose a challenge when you're an entertainer and you have partners who don't want to feel like a secret.

Yet I've learned, especially over these past few years in my dynamic with my son's father, Darius, it's inappropriate when people feel they have access to your private relationships. And as an entertainer, it's never just brothers, moms, and dads giving unsolicited advice, but also random people online. It's even more unsettling when one person has not spent most of their life understanding the unique parasocial relationship between a performer and their audience. The public will always operate as the audience. And the audience loves a good show.

The persona who you know as Keke Palmer has been how I've moved through this world. My introverted self created an extroverted persona to allow the real me to exist in my own personal comfort and vice versa. And I do understand that my extroverted self feels very real to y'all, because she is very real since she is a part of me. But there's the part of me that I'm comfortable with the world seeing, and there's the part of me that I keep reserved and tucked backstage. The people who are closest to me see something different in Lauren, and they know the work I've done to create these lines so nothing gets blurred, as they've been with me all my life as I figured it out.

So the truth is that my son's father didn't realize I was holding a boundary between the audience and me. Let me be clear: I trust the audience as the audience, especially when it comes to sacred things. I'm very aware of who I am and who I am to those watching because

I've entertained all my life. I love being a clown, but it does hurt when y'all laugh while I'm not performing.

I'm here for entertainment and I have no problem with that. I'm very clear on what our relationship is in that regard. On every level, I'm there as something to be presented. And that doesn't mean I'm not being authentic in that, but it does mean I must always have my personal boundary with myself of what my expectations are of you. And what my expectations are of me, and what I should give to you. These are boundaries I've worked years to establish with myself.

When everything went down, Usher told me, "No one can tell you what to perform, control your own narrative. I know, I've been doing this since I was a kid and you, too. When you dedicate your life to this, a lot of the time people forget what you have created is just that. An image, an idea, a performance. Even sometimes people that we date, sometimes they forget we're entertainers, because they see such a different side of us." Which is absolutely true. I feel that's what happened to me because the reaction I got from Darius seeing me onstage was unexpected. And I guess if you're any good at entertaining it would feel interchangeable with the real you. Like, every bit should feel like it could be real. Interesting how a good performance can make life at home hard.

Then there's that dual conflict where it doesn't matter that I'm a performer, the question is "Do you love me, or is that, too, a performance?" I don't know what it's like to date a performer, but I would imagine it could be triggering knowing someone everyone thinks they know better than you do. Like a ventriloquist dummy on a shelf that looks so real you have to pull it apart to prove it's just a toy. Well, I'm human. I go through human things. I have flaws. But I won't let anyone pull my strings to prove that fact. Instead, I will pull my own strings, thank you very much, until I decide to rest on a shelf. Or get out of the elevator.

I love the craft, I love the art, and I'm committed to the veil and the protection I have in existing in a performative nature that I created *before* I became famous. But sometimes our close ones forget that people don't get what's going on, and not only do people not get what's going on, but they're also not supposed to. I don't need the audience to know that I put gold in the pudding, babes. They love the taste, that's all that matters. And I feel this way about love; my duty to show that is to that person, not the audience. And personal happiness is all that matters.

So the talk doesn't deter me because the world knows me as an entertainer. And I do give y'all the real me, but y'all don't *know* the real me. Because you can never really know someone who you've watched from a distance all your life.

At the time I couldn't even really process everything I'm sharing now. So looking back and having the time to reflect on what happened has given me a newfound sense of clarity. The mental distance was necessary. And, for me, I know this person that I had this child with in a way that no one is ever really gonna understand. Unless they have a child with them, and maybe even then they wouldn't understand it. So here it is that I have this person who I am at odds with, who understands me and who I understand in a way that other people won't. Does it hurt that it became a nightmare? Absolutely. But I know that life goes on. I know I'm not the only person who has been called out by a partner online, or has found themselves in unhealthy relationship dynamics, or has dealt with a breakup just a few months postpartum. These are things that happen to people, and I'm not ashamed. I just know that my *work* isn't about those things.

When the audience thinks I'm the joke, honey, we've lost the plot. The plot is about a young, beautiful Black girl from the south suburbs of Chicago who uprooted her life and her family, who created a brand and created a business, who spent years becoming a generational talent. That's the plot. It's not "I've got problems with my baby daddy."

Now, let's move on.

MASTER OF ME
SELF-ASSESSMENT EXERCISE

Hold up, wait a minute! I've got some exercises to help you remember the important stuff, so you can easily recall it later. Consider it a pit stop on our journey together—a chance to reflect and get ready for what's next!

1. **What happens when an artist's purpose becomes overly identified with their performance?**
    a) They lose sight of their true self
    b) They gain more control over their message
    c) They become more confident in their abilities
    d) They disconnect from their audience

2. **What is the benefit of practicing healthy detachment in the workplace?**
    a) Losing one's identity
    b) Gaining more recognition
    c) Having more creative freedom
    d) Becoming more objective

3. **What can happen when the audience's expectations drive your performance?**
    a) You gain more creative freedom
    b) You lose sight of your artistic vision
    c) You become more confident in your abilities
    d) You disconnect from your audience

4. **What's the risk of prioritizing your message over your own well-being?**
    a) You become more resilient
    b) You lose sight of your own needs
    c) You gain more recognition
    d) You disconnect from your audience

(Turn the page to see the answers!)

ANSWER KEY

1. ANSWER: A) THEY LOSE SIGHT OF THEIR TRUE SELF

REFLECT: Purpose can be a part of your job but it doesn't have to be the job. What does fulfilling your purpose look like disconnected from financial gain?

COUNTERACT: To avoid losing yourself in your performance, try setting boundaries between your onstage and offstage personas. Prioritize self-care and engage in activities that bring you joy outside your art.

2. ANSWER: D) BECOMING MORE OBJECTIVE

REFLECT: Has there been a time where you took something personally at work that interrupted your ability to do the job? What would you have done differently to exercise detachment?

COUNTERACT: To maintain objectivity, remind yourself that your primary purpose at work is to perform your job duties and achieve your professional goals. You are there to:
- Complete tasks and deliver results
- Earn a living to support your wider pursuits and passions
- Develop skills and expertise

Avoid getting distracted by seeking validation or friendship from your job or colleagues. Instead, focus on:
- Setting clear boundaries
- Prioritizing your tasks and goals
- Maintaining a professional demeanor
- Keeping your personal and professional lives separate

3. ANSWER: B) YOU LOSE SIGHT OF YOUR ARTISTIC VISION

REFLECT: Have you ever felt pressured by audience expectations? How did you handle it?

COUNTERACT: To maintain your artistic vision, prioritize your own creative needs and desires. Set clear boundaries with your audience and stakeholders, and engage in self-reflection to ensure you're staying true to your art.

4. ANSWER: B) YOU LOSE SIGHT OF YOUR OWN NEEDS

REFLECT: Have you ever prioritized your message over your own well-being? What were the consequences?

COUNTERACT: To maintain your well-being, prioritize self-care and engage in activities that bring you joy outside your art. Set realistic goals and boundaries, and seek support from loved ones and peers.

OPEN-ENDED QUESTIONS

- What are some moments in your life when you felt like you were "performing" or trying to meet others' expectations? How did that feel?
- Where in your life are you currently carrying the burden of perfection? What would happen if you released that weight?
- In what ways are you "pulling your own strings" and making intentional choices? Where might you need more self-awareness and agency?
- How have you been conditioned to seek external validation or approval? What small steps can you take to cultivate self-acceptance and authenticity?
- What would it look like for you to embrace your unique journey and let go of comparisons to or competition with others?

KEY TAKEAWAYS

- Embrace authenticity
- Perfection is a burden
- Self-awareness is power

"Visualize yourself not falling off the wall."

Part II
POWER

[phonetic: **pou**-er]

noun

1. ability to do or act; capability of doing or accomplishing something:
   > Everyone has the power to better themselves.

   Synonyms: *capacity*

   Antonyms: *incapacity*

2. political or national strength:
   > The Second World War changed the balance of power in Europe.

3. great or marked ability to do or act; <u>strength</u>; <u>might</u>; <u>force</u>.

   Synonyms: *energy*

   Antonyms: *weakness*

4. the possession of control or command over people; <u>authority</u>; <u>influence</u>: *Words have tremendous power over our minds.*[2]

---

2 "power," *Dictionary.com*, 2024, https://www.dictionary.com.

PODCAST CLIP: BUILDING A MEDIA EMPIRE WITH TYLER PERRY

Keke Palmer: I remember being in Chicago.

Oh my gosh. I remember going to my uncle's and aunt's house and they're like, "Have y'all seen the new Tyler Perry play?" And they'll put it on and we're watching it. It was just insane. And I actually use the model that you had of, you know, your work already existing and being big and you having that kind of proof, that data, and being able to empower yourself in the film industry. I used a lot of that when I had to revamp my career, you know, from being a child entertainer and reaching this moment where everybody was kind of like, "Okay, you've grown up, this is what we see for you. If you're not going to fit into this box, then that's that."

So I turned to digital, you know, it wasn't necessarily stage shows, but I chose digital as a way to produce my own work and kind of set the stage for who I wanted to be. And if you want to get a part of that, then you can. Because look, I have this audience and they're rocking with me. So either jump on board or not.

And something I wanted to point out as well was when you started working with Lionsgate, I read that you had a deal that they would coproduce and distribute the films, but you would retain all copyright ownership. That's everything. Oh my gosh, I think that is such an important thing when we're having this conversation about ownership and entrepreneurship and what intellectual property means to the creator.

How did you know to do that? And how hard did you have to fight for it?

Tyler Perry: I, it wasn't a fight for me because it was a nonnegotiable. I was not going to negotiate with anybody about that. And because I had that audience that had been with me, who had made me pretty wealthy going into Hollywood, I didn't need them.

I was selling DVDs from my website at the time and they were bootlegged everywhere, but then people were, people were finding them, but, but I wasn't to, to give up ownership is a nonnegotiable because what happens is I know what that does for, for your future. And for your power and for what? It's the difference in waiting for somebody to give you a job or knowing that a check is gonna be in the mailbox, whether you have a job or not.

So I wanted to build this legacy and, and, and for my son and my future, even though I didn't know he was coming at the time, but also watching Oprah own her show. It was, it was that example that are like, *Oh, well, what does that mean? She owns a show. Wait, wait, wait. That's what that means.* So even from the beginning, when I was doing the stage shows, like my name had to be on the marquee and my name had to be on the tickets and the promoters were getting mad.

"Who's this kid think he is? Why are you putting it?" I was building a brand. I knew that in order to build that people have to remember the name. In order for you to stand out, you've got to have something that they remember. It all started from my father, who worked for a white man building houses—I say white man for a reason—worked for a white man building houses and he was a subcontractor. So on the weekend he'd get his eight hundred dollars and he'd be so happy he got paid. But I watched a white guy sell the house for, for eighty thousand dollars. I'm like, "Why won't you take the money and build your own house and sell it." Him and my mother coming from a Jim Crow South, they didn't think that. They would tell me that kind of thing is for white folks. They can't do it. But everything in me was going, *That's not true. I can own the house, too.* So that's what this is about. Owning the house and building it from that point of view.

KP: How did you tap into knowing that, right? Because we can, we can hear these things and we can feel these ways, but the action that you put behind it and the follow-through is what makes the difference.

Was this the people that you surrounded yourself with? Were you reading? You know, what was that that made you know that those are the steps you had to take?

TP: All I can tell you for me, I have a divine leading grace on my life that I call the grace of God. That I just follow. If it doesn't feel right, I don't do it.

I was like, *That doesn't feel right. Let me go this direction.* Or, and I've, I've had agents in Hollywood be really upset with me because I wanted, wouldn't do this. "Do you know how much money—" That's not what I want to do. That doesn't feel right. I'm going to go this way. "Tyler, that's—" And they would always tell me, "That's not going to work."

Like with *House of Payne*, you know, when I went to, to do the episodes, they said, "Only do one, a pilot, we'll shop it around." It's like, no, I feel like I need to do ten. I'm going to do ten. So I did these first ten, they sat in a can for, uh, ever. And nobody wanted them. And then UPN and WB, or WB and one of them, they became the CW. There was a merger. All the affiliates were without programming. So they started calling around. What do you have? Somebody said, "This guy in Atlanta's got these ten episodes." They put it on. The ratings were higher than what was there before. So it was like being prepared. Right? So I have constantly in, in prayer, I want to be prepared for what's coming next.

What is the next moment that's coming? I want to be clear about it. Like when I built my first studio, by the time I got to this one I'm in now, when I saw it, I thought if I had seen it first, I would be like, *This is too much land*. But I learned to build for where I was going and not where I was. So all of these things happened in progress as I was, as I was growing and working.

And paying attention to everything. To everything.

6

AIN'T THAT 'BOUT A BITCH?

I was never afraid of my power. In all honesty, deep down, I've always liked everything about myself. The problem always resided in the way other people responded to me that made me feel a level of discomfort. My confidence, my voice, my unapologetic self can be perceived as a threat to those who are used to seeing people like me in a more subdued light. Just because I saw myself as confident and strong didn't mean others would see me the same way—their perceptions were often filtered through their own biases and expectations. I was often met with this energy where others tried to diminish me or make me question my reality because it wasn't always—and still isn't—the one society told me to live in. It's true that people will feel the need to harbor this competitive energy with you when you want nothing more than to simply exist. All because it challenges their reality and the unnecessary limits they're putting on themselves.

After years of being unable to articulate the problem, I've come to realize that the struggle isn't with self-acceptance but with the discomfort others project onto us. We absorb their insecurities and stereotypes, making it hard to see our own worth. It's not that we don't like ourselves, but that we're constantly bombarded with messages telling us we're not enough or that our value lies in meeting certain standards. The problem isn't that you are short or tall or Black or white or light or dark or whatever! The problem lies in social constructs and how what's of value fluctuates. For example, you may think you want a big butt, or big lips, or long hair, but really, you just want to be seen as beautiful. Beauty is not limited to those things, but when they're constantly pushed as desirable, it becomes hard to hold on to that truth.

I don't know why but I've always looked beyond the surface level, spotting the unique qualities that make each person special. Perhaps my experience with character work has sharpened my observational and acceptance skills. Regardless of how others may judge someone, I can find something that makes them awesome. It's not about ignoring flaws or shortcomings, but about recognizing there are multiple perspectives that bring beauty in everyone's distinct story. This ability to see the good in others has shaped me into the person I am today, and it's brought me more joy than harm.

My true power outside of knowing who I am is encouraging others and being an example of how others can own who they are, too. The faith it took for me to overcome the challenges of people telling me to question who I am took a lot of soul-searching. I truly spent a lot of time talking to myself and getting past the surface emotions to get to the root of my issues. A lot of times we stop at "I don't like my [blank]." For me, I'll be honest and say that "blank" is my skin. The issue isn't solely the fact that I have acne; yes, that's annoying on a superficial level, but the true fixation that lies within it is the idea that I can fix everything in my life and that there is always a solution, but when it comes to this one thing, there is not. This led me to my problem of needing to be in control, which is a conversation for another day. My point is, asking ourselves enough questions leads us to what we are actually running up against, which offers the clarity to know how to deal with it.

Time and time again, different relationships with romantic partners and platonic friends made me unsure of who I thought I was, but what I did find was my authenticity through those experiences. And I made sure to be gentle with myself through difficult times. Knowing ourselves is never a done deal because we're always evolving as individuals in this ever-changing world, but it's truly about accepting ourselves at every stage of this journey and not resisting who we are becoming or will become.

Let me tell you: playing small doesn't serve the world. Own your power! It's actually more dangerous when we do not. When we play small and pretend that we aren't capable, especially when people look to us to be capable, that's when we unintentionally create chaos. Surrendering to not knowing is one thing, that's powerful because it allows you the space to find out. But knowing and pretending not to out of fear of what will be expected of you is what I'm referring to. The chaos one lives in is an expression of the chaos coming from the inner conflict they have about how powerful they are. When we actively choose ourselves, we are in a state of acceptance and that's peace.

There's a moment during *Homecoming* towards the end of her performance when Beyoncé makes an announcement. She appears at the top of the bleachers above her band and dancers. She looks out into the crowd and says, "Thank you for allowing me to be the first Black woman to headline Coachella." Then she pauses. The camera pans across the many faces of the BeyHive as they cheer her on. They're screaming so loud you might think you're there, too! The energy they're releasing is the same energy that we've watched the performers onstage embody all night long.

Beyoncé cocks an eyebrow and continues, "Ain't that 'bout a bitch?" Her facial expression says it all; she's surprised, but she's unsurprised. Then she launches into her iconic song "Run the World (Girls)." I love this moment for many reasons. Not just because she looks flawless on this stage after performing for over an hour (sorcery!), but it's also her acknowledgment of the trailblazers who came before her. As she highlights her significance breaking this barrier in Coachella's nearly twenty-year history, she expresses her gratitude to the women who've opened the doors before her, and she continues to execute her talents onstage.

There are several recent headlines that acknowledge women who continue to shatter these glass ceilings. In 2022, Ketanji Brown Jackson made history as the first Black woman appointed to the United States Supreme Court. In 2023, Halle Bailey became the first Black woman to be cast in a Disney live-action remake when she played the role of Ariel in *The Little Mermaid*. In 2024, Lily Gladstone was the first Native American to be nominated for an Oscar for Best Actress. The list goes on.

I've been the first (or the youngest) at many things, and I cheer for myself as much as I cheer for the next person. Whether I am the first Black woman to win the Emmy for Outstanding Game Show Host for *Password* or as the youngest talk show host, I'm basking in all these accomplishments. You know why? Because I worked my ass off for these moments!

I've had people ask me about what it meant to me to be "the first," typically with a sullen expression. I absolutely understand the frustration and the need to feel disappointed in these institutions for being late in their recognition—hell, I am, too! But to hear the initial reaction "I don't think it's good to be the first" upon hearing historic cultural news gives me quite the jump scare. It's almost like, why shouldn't we reframe this and be excited that somebody is the first? Because that means they're trailblazing and they're breaking down doors and so on. At times the backlash to being the first rings so loud it seems to undercut the person's accomplishments.

It's not their fault that they're the first. Usually, another person is breaking down a door that we didn't even know needed to be broken. Go ahead, sister! Go ahead, brother! It's a good thing, so talk your shit! And I mean, yeah, we can talk about how far behind we are from actual progress in America, but I mean, guys, we already know that. You know what I mean? We know these systems are unfair to minorities and people from historically marginalized backgrounds. We already know that America loves capitalism and benefits off the invisible work of non-white people. I'm the kind of person for whom it's like, there is no being surprised at this point. If there's anything that we should be exhausted by, it should be being surprised by systemic racism and the underlying societal conflict as it pertains to race, sexuality, creed, gender, age, and so on and so forth. Beyoncé said it best: "Ain't that 'bout a bitch?" Then she didn't miss a beat. Glass ceilings continued to shatter.

What I'm saying is, I don't know if we're gonna change anything by not showing up for those who've initially pushed through those doors. Let's cheer for them instead of being annoyed and saying, "Wowwww." Now, I'm not saying we shouldn't discuss it every now and then, but at what vantage point are we discussing it from? And is that sentiment louder than the sound of your claps for the trailblazer? I'll be honest, I don't know about you, but I can't cry about it anymore. I've done that and I've harbored resentment for weeks at a time, but I have no more tears left. I only know how to find a solution to it, for me and for my life. If the door's not opening, I'm gonna bulldoze through it. By any means necessary, you know what I mean? I can't give more energy into why it's the first door that's being bulldozed through. I just know I'm gonna take those doors down and I'm also gonna take whoever the fuck wanna come with me. And that's how I step into my power.

When I hear someone say something like, "The world sucks, so I can't really do what I want to do or be who I want to be because it's so shitty here," it's like, nice try, but let's be better than that. Let's really challenge ourselves to clean up our own backyards rather than focusing on all the things going awry in our neighbor's shitty garden. I call this a very sophisticated version of procrastination, or covert narcissism disguised as altruism, as my girl Taylor Swift would say. I'm not saying we can't help each other, I'm just saying we have to be sure that we don't use focusing on others as a way to avoid ourselves. There is more pride in being the change you want to see rather than commenting negatively on other people being the change that they want to see.

And the truth is you will never know all that had to be done for this person to get to that point in their career. You may be the first [insert marginalized identity] in the C-suite at your company, or the first [insert marginalized identity] valedictorian in your school's history, or even the first in your family to graduate from college. That's a huge accomplishment. And I'm proud of you. It's a win. And a win is a win, honey. As long as we remember that the first shouldn't be the only, and we continue to be the best in our respective fields regardless of our accolades. Because anything other than doing what you consider your best work will feel like a distraction. Trust me.

Let me share this gem. Once upon a time, I found myself gravitating towards these words by Toni Morrison:

> The function, the very serious function of racism is distraction. It keeps you from doing your work. It keeps you explaining, over and over again, your reason for being. Somebody says you have no language and you spend twenty years proving that you do. Somebody says your head isn't shaped properly so you have scientists working on the fact that it is. Somebody says you have no art so you dredge that up. Somebody says you have no kingdoms, so you dredge that up. None of this is necessary. There will always be one more thing.

Every few years, people call out colorism in the industry, and one time I came up in the conversation. I was being compared to someone

I know and it was such a strange thing to go on Twitter and see our faces next to each other, with our names trending in relation to this and not a remake of *Bride Wars* (start the paperwork)! It made me think about how often we're measured against others and how surreal it is to see ourselves through the eyes of strangers. People were reposting and arguing on a few different threads for hours.

First of all, she and I are as alike as Halle Berry and Angela Bassett. We're two different types of entertainers, two totally different perspectives. The only thing that is similar is that we both started out as kid actors on Disney, but didn't Ryan Gosling start out as a kid actor on Disney, too? Why wasn't anyone comparing my career to his? People decided because of her proximity to whiteness that she'd had a better career than me.... It's a constant reminder that, no matter how successful I become, my worth will always be tied to my skin tone in some people's eyes (heavy on *some*). That's basically Colorism 101 and it's pretty exhausting. Because in what world does my career need to be compared to hers? And how, in any way, am I not successful? I shouldn't be compared to somebody period, and especially not just because they're of a lighter skin tone. Skin complexion shouldn't inflate or deflate someone's merit. Comparisons, to me, are unnecessary in general because to compare would mean you and that person have the same goal. How can you compare people who have two totally different goals? How can you compare people who use different approaches to achieve their goals? How can you compare people when you don't even know where *you're* going, let alone where they are going? Chileeee.

And when I look back on this moment, it was such an interesting take to me. *Nope* was just hitting theaters and the news that it hit $100 million at the domestic box office was insane. I was celebrating and feeling good that this movie was connecting with audiences. It was also my first movie going number one in this new, not-really-post-but-post-pandemic era where everyone knew that the state of movie tickets was still low-key in flux. It was not only a career milestone but also a moment of pride and validation for me and my community. It supported the fact that our stories matter, and our voices deserve to be heard and celebrated on the biggest stages, through its success. So here I am, starring in a movie where I'm literally playing a heroine with one of the biggest directors—Black or white—of our generation. But I got people telling me my career isn't as good as someone else's because of the complexion of my skin? No, babe, I won't let you project that onto me. Because it's actually a lie. I'm actually extraordinarily successful, getting everything I wanna get, and I'm not dead yet.

Like, damn, y'all killed me. My career ain't even over; how can I be underrated at thirty? I just got put in the big girl oven—like, let me cook!

I am literally a Black woman playing a role and a character that are typically reserved for men. I'm playing this queer-identifying woman and I'm bouncing around the film with my natural hair that's giving cute, kinky, curly afro. The greatest director of my era has just put a movie on the map that eventually earned over $180 million and it's not an IP that has already been used. It's new at a time when no one is taking a chance on anything that isn't Marvel, DC, damn near Star Wars! I really don't think we should be comparing me to anybody, because there are more important things to be talking about. I wanted to pop up on social media and tune in to conversations about the film's innovative synthesis of modern Western tropes and Black American cultural iconography, or the film's subtle messages about our addiction to spectacle as humans. Hell, the conversations could've even been a color analysis about the mysterious flying alien that literally had us running and ducking all over the place and I would've been more impressed.

The most dangerous thing to me was how divisive things got, especially within our community. These projected assumptions and ideas that, let's be honest, originated over four hundred years ago were falsehoods that were meant to separate us and perpetuate the notion that our value and worth are based on our proximity to whiteness. We know the role colorism plays and what it's rooted in. And these assumptions have always been dangerous because they bothered me as a kid, too.

And we know that there's a certain superficial advantage; our society says that certain things are more valuable than most. And that's ultimately what I think we see acted out, whether in our personal lives, our relationships, or whatever. It's really about wanting to be of value, not actually being unhappy with who you are or what you have. But wanting that to be a given and not something you have to overexert to prove. However, this creates a self-perpetuating cycle where, no matter your accomplishments, societal biases will always undermine your worth, leaving you feeling like you're never enough. There was never a time I looked in the mirror and didn't like myself. But you know what I didn't like? I didn't like that people wanted me to not like myself. Why is the world perceiving someone to have more than me or be better than me based on the shade of my Blackness? I really hated that, and I think it's because as a kid I was quite arrogant. 'Cause I was a cute-ass kid! I looked at myself like, "I'm everything."

Colorism, racism, sexism, and all the *-isms* will always exist. To me, if you and your partner or loved ones are really aware of what that means at the core, then it shouldn't really bother you. And I think that's the same in families, in relationships, in the workplace. But you can and should always speak up on ignorance. Because ignorance is not necessarily "You're stupid," but to my understanding, it's almost more like you bought in on the lie. And if you haven't bought in on the lie, then you can actually see things quite clearly and understand what these constructs are and how they play into the value system.

The situation on Twitter got so bad that people were doing all this stuff like searching online net worths—which, if you didn't know, are not real. And then people were being critical of the other woman's work, saying she wasn't good, or she got roles because of her proximity to whiteness, so it's like everything she'd done was solely based on how she looks and not her hard work. I hated all of it.

I really wanted to handle it with grace because it's not to say that colorism doesn't exist, but I didn't think my career was an example of that. In actuality, it's an example of the opposite because people do come seeking out women who look like me. I decided to hit 'em with a quick tweet:

> A great example of colorism is to believe I can be compared to anyone. I'm the youngest talk show host ever. The first Black woman to star in her own show on Nickelodeon, & the youngest & first Black Cinderella on broadway. I'm an incomparable talent. Baby, THIS, is Keke Palmer.

Ultimately, what I was trying to get across was that I wanted people to stop limiting themselves, which was being projected in their view of me. Because when the conversation evolved into what it evolved into, I was like, Damn! Maybe I'm the one who has to go back to the drawing board and figure out how to respond to this in a way that can support my desire to make people turn inward. Because if me achieving the greatest accomplishments of my life thus far, existing as a Black woman, isn't enough for you, then I'm like—fuck! I've got to figure out how to really translate this message, because I thought just achieving said enough.

I was really having internal conversations with myself during this whole Twitter debacle. *Okay sooo, even in my being amazing, you're still finding it hard to believe that despite what society told you, I'm still out here doing the most?* And I really do think this is the same thing that any Black person who represents the culture in this way is always up against. Because our hope and our desire (or at least I can speak for myself) are that seeing it is enough. We can't solve much of anything, but at least we can give hope and push the needle just a smidge forward for those watching, who can then add on, and so forth.

Seeing Brandy do it was enough for me. Seeing Oprah do it was enough for me. It's always been enough for me. But then there came a certain point when, for certain people, it was still not enough, and I was trying to understand why. I think it's hard to make it out of that mental hole if you don't look to those you admire, whoever they are for you, who pushed against the grain and made it through. There are enough societal viruses in our minds that put these limits on us.

I think about how people were always quick to say that so-and-so is part of the Illuminati. Insert huge groan. Now, obviously, there's some eerie shit that goes on in life. But if everybody who succeeds who you don't think should be succeeding is in the Illuminati, then you gotta look inward, beau. You *gotta* look inward. Because everybody is not in the Illuminati now, and what it means is you don't believe that people can succeed for real. That means you believe there's a ceiling for them, and if they've gone past that ceiling, they must be part of the Illuminati or something equally sinister.

At the same time, it's so terrible when people use your success against the people around you. They turn your blessings into another person's "inadequacy." I see these conversations often in the R&B scene, where so many incredible, talented people have done so much for us to have the best love songs to vibe out to and people still try to say that genre is dead. The worst part is that these conversations will all be out of your control; there's literally nothing you can do about it but let people talk! What I know now is that people will project their insecurities onto you because in your successes are *their* inadequacies. Simply put: PEOPLE BE JEALOUS OF YOU. Many times, they don't even realize they're being envious. They see your talent; they see the way you shine and they don't know how you do it, so they try to tamper it down. The only way they can interfere is to make you feel less than, and there is no better way to do that to someone than to compare them to someone else: "Well, they ain't doing good as so-and-so."

At the end of the day, I do genuinely want people to see the greatness in themselves and shine light onto others in the process. I don't want to be idolized. I want to be a teacher. I want to be someone who helps to guide you there; I want to be a representation of a path undisturbed. I'm doing what I'm doing because I love it, but also because I know there's a greater purpose to all this. I feel like that's what God put me here for, and, you know, everybody's not spiritual and that's fine. But even if you're not religious, or if you don't have a relationship with a higher power, I know that I'm here for a good reason. And that's not just to argue with people on Twitter.

I don't believe we're just here to fuck around for the sake of doing so. I truly do believe that we're meant to connect, and we're meant to do stuff that affects our experience here in a good way, while also being able to encourage each other and lead by example. And so, for me, behind the scenes, I take all this quite seriously. It becomes so hard and difficult, even when it doesn't feel personal. Even in you representing, showing, and working twice as hard to be the things that people are afraid to see. Or maybe the things they don't want to see.

The truth is everybody doesn't have to like what you do for you to be successful with it. It really doesn't matter who hates it; what really matters more is who likes it. There is an audience for everything, so please keep doing your thing.

I think this is so important to remember because so many people have opinions. Nowhere does it say that everyone has to love you for your business to thrive. In fact, many people make successful businesses out of people hating them. Never allow your value to be subject to *taste*. Being "good" and "entertaining" is quite subjective. I have experienced this so many times in my life and in so many ways. And at some point, people just realize you know who you are and you have your own vision. You can't help but respect consistency and self-acceptance. Some shit ain't for you. And that's okay!

So please understand this on your continued ride to greatness. And remember: any time someone tries to use another person as a comparative marker for where you are or where you're supposed to be, cut they asses loose!

7
AMERICA, WE HAVE A PROBLEM

Corporations are gonna corporate. I had to come to terms with the fact that the entertainment industry is really just like any other industry. In this country, every industry across the board is dealing with employees who are being overworked, underpaid, and undervalued.

I can only speak from an entertainer's perspective when I say that we run businesses to keep our brands afloat; "we" being both the brand and the business. What I mean by that is that the businesses that keep our brands "branding" are made up of employees. That would be a publicist, stylists for hair and makeup, a manager, an agent, and maybe an assistant or a CMO, depending on if you're Will Smith–ing it. Some of these people are paid by percentage and others are paid a salary. These employees can greatly decrease any assumed large lump sum. It's like on *Shark Tank*, when the "sharks" ask you what your cost-to-earn ratio is. Sometimes, as entertainers, we have to invest more in our brand without knowing how we will get the return. In the words of the late great Notorious B.I.G., "More money, more problems."

Sometimes I feel like people assume that everybody in the industry is stacked with all this cash, but y'all gotta understand: To make money, you must spend money. So what seems like a lot is taken by even more. There is still privilege in this depending on your perspective and what vantage point you're seeing this from. It's like saying you get $100 and I only get $50, but what it takes to get me $100 costs me $50. This is a poor example of trying to explain how things are neutralized for us in our business because of what it takes to stay in our business. It's not like we just come to work and get paid—maybe someone does, but for me and most of my friends, we had to spend so much money on marketing and jump through so many hoops to even be seen. On the outside it seems like we are making more than we need, and maybe that's true for some, but with any business, what you earn is only as good as what you invest. Almost like gambling, right? Like you made more because you spent more, but you had more to spend and that's the place we are all wanting to get to. To financially have the room to gamble on ourselves and put ourselves in the positions that no one else will.

This is why no one can really have one job anymore! Someone working outside the entertainment industry may also do Uber Eats, or Postmates, or they may be a part-time accountant, or a substitute teacher every other week just to gain multiple streams of income.

For an entertainment career you might be like me: an actor, influencer, host, singer, speaker, etc. I keep a job because I *have* to! We *all* work multiple jobs, and we may like some more than others, but we also do them because we have to. How else are we supposed to keep the lights on? Everyone's idea of success is different because success is subjective, but to be fiscally "successful" and live in America means learning the delicate dance with your cash-to-expense ratio. And this is why entrepreneurship is so important and complex, yet being an entrepreneur in itself is hella expensive! Having one job is not really an option for anyone no matter what industry you're in. Unless you're like the top, top, top, TOP earner, and I'm talking Bill Gates and them, I suppose. I don't know, I surely can't relate! Why do you think they call me Keke "Keep a Bag" Palmer? I's workin'!

I'm not complaining or trying to draw comparisons, but I do acknowledge that we all have similar struggles in our industries because corporations run everything, and they aren't necessarily for the people. Corporations are gonna corporate.

The conversations around retirement due to burnout are really real. And I also don't think people, as the audience, realize how much they are playing into some of the critical turmoil that an artist has to face, which is that you guys don't really want the show to end. (I know Rihanna wearing that "I'm Retired" shirt was a jump scare for everyone online, but look at how many articles and headlines came out about that *one* shirt—which she was surely joking about ... Right, Rih?)

And, if I'm being honest, I end up having so many conflicting feelings about some of these conversations within the industry because the monetary aspect has never really overly moved me. I'm more interested in looking at things from a business perspective, because what really happens when you make a case and say that you're worth *x* amount because of your talent, and who you are as an individual, and yet the project you've been working on isn't even considered a marginal success to your own managers? In fact, it doesn't really do any of the things that would be necessary to justify what you've asked for. Now it feels like we're avoiding being truthful about the business and how to actually leverage proper business opportunities. It's like mixing apples and oranges together to make an apple pie, but it tastes like crap because you can't use oranges to make an apple pie!

I really do feel the actual conversation for younger people, and any artist out there, should be that if you want more opportunities, and better business opportunities, you should diversify your portfolio and leverage your other businesses against the ones you want to get more from. That's why I started hosting! And I mean, yes, there was a personal desire, because I do love talking to people and hosting fulfills this inner-child feeling that I've always kept inside me, but if I can talk to people, make incredible connections, and get paid while doing so—why the hell not?

Take a moment to really think about it right now. My question to you is: What are your personal desires?

There's a real pushback on hustle culture because our country isn't the same anymore. Blame corporatism; it's simply not the same anymore. Everybody's got headquarters now. Even the banks got a headquarters and it's the damn federal bank. So this idea that we're gonna beat the system—I hate to say it, I hope I don't sound ridiculous—is futile. Rather than trying to beat the system, we should focus on mastering ourselves. As systems continually evolve, self-mastery allows us to remain adaptable and fluid, turning upheaval into opportunity. It's about knowing what you like, what you're good at, and using that as leverage against the system so that it works for you.

Invest in yourself. Make your own films. Go on tour. Put out your own stuff. If you don't want to work with and for corporations, try to make it a reality that you won't! Something I learned from watching the career of Aziz Ansari is that he didn't have to worry about people not wanting to do the movies that he wanted to do and that he doesn't have to worry about playing roles he doesn't want to play. Because he can do his stand-up! He can go out there, say whatever the fuck he wants to say on that stage, and make a sizable paycheck that he can then put into his own thing—if that's what he wants to do.

So the conversation about begging and beating down the doors of corporations—it can only go so far. You know? You can only control so much. We can only strike so much until so many of us are broken and burned-out. So many people in my industry took real hits to their wallets (and, by the way, it wasn't the people who could afford to take these hits). The people who were fighting for something, those were the people who ended up suffering. So we gotta come up with a new plan, because, y'all, I can't get behind anything that's gonna leave us with empty pockets, fighting for something that rich people have no problem taking. I'm serious!

I gotta be a logical earth sign, because it ain't gonna work, babes. Maybe I'm stubborn, but I don't believe that's gonna move the needle. What will move the needle is you knowing what your value is, knowing what your personal power is, and leveraging those things so you can get what you want, or so you can decide to not be a part of the things you don't want to be a part of. And what do I mean by leveraging your personal power? I mean spreading yourself out into many spaces. Letting go of the college idea that you have to pick one major and picking many things and seeing how they pan out. Which, if you stick with them all to a certain degree, will all pan out eventually. Then what you learn from one you can take to the other, and that creates value that only you have. When it came to hosting, I had already been performing for most of my life at a high level. I had done some hosting in my career through just pure promotions of TV shows and films because, of course, the Disney machine. Even though my career was not in the place it had been at its height, I was still an unexpected person for my age and had the popularity to be on daytime television. So what was not at the time valued in the traditional acting and TV space made me more valuable in the hosting space.

So let's consider what it looks like to diversify our portfolios and create some tangible, realistic options for ourselves.

I remember having a similar conversation with Boots Riley, who said, "I [would] have no problem living in my car if it meant I was able to make the things I wanted to make." And, as people, we have to be real with that and have those honest conversations about how far we are willing to go and where we draw the line and how each choice informs the kind of career we will have. I know in my heart of hearts that I'd rather file for bankruptcy before I do things that compromise my integrity or make me feel bad. But I have done, and do sometimes do, things I don't really *need* to do on a passion-type level only because they're going to allow me the freedom to do the things I really want to do.

And this is truly the kind of negotiating that I have with myself on a daily freaking basis. It's a conversation I have to have every day, and I want people to understand that there's no world in personal or business life where you get what you want the exact way you want. It's like politics. And although I hate the casualness of the lesser-of-two-evils gag, we always would have to go with a flawed but not too annoyingly flawed candidate because nothing and no one is ever 100 percent the "vibe." Sometimes you have to bend a little and that's okay. Be water, like Bruce Lee said, fluid and flexible. Because perfection is a lie! A big part of mastering yourself is not being so delulu in thinking that there's gonna be some big offer that's gonna come if you just hold on tight. Sometimes holding on tight means nothing good gets in. Sometimes holding on tight is just what we hide behind when we don't know how to collaborate with not only others but our journey with ourselves and manifesting our dreams in this material world. That in itself is a contradiction, so we must create space for it to happen the way it can happen, within reason. Every day of your life is gonna be—and should be—a negotiation.

I know we can outsmart the system, but we've also got to start out smart *in* the system. And that doesn't mean less work, honey. It actually does mean more work. Way more work. But the benefit you get from that is the freedom to say no, which is really big. I often think about artists who've successfully acquired their music masters, and how this ownership plays into their legacies. Nowadays you can't talk about Jay-Z, Taylor Swift, or Rihanna without considering how they've fought to maintain their musical legacies. And it's always been a struggle for artists because the music industry is its own beast. If you say Scooter Braun three times, you might be able to summon him in your bathroom mirror. (Kidding!)

I remember when Queen Latifah was starting to produce her own movies for Netflix, and what she was offering to pay me was lower than I'd expected, but I knew I wanted to learn from her. I also knew that she was going to allow me to be a producer on the project and she was somebody I wanted to have a continued relationship with, so I was 100 percent on board. She's always been a mentor to me and opportunities like that were pretty rare for someone like me in general. The material was fun, thoughtful, and exciting, and I thought it would be a great piece of work to give to my fans. So I did that project, and *Brotherly Love* became a fan favorite. I gained a producing credit because I was emerging as a young person and starting to produce my own stuff. It was something I could put in my portfolio.

My gratitude from that experience was through the roof, and it showed. When Queen Latifah started on the next job, she raised my quote. So even though she gave me a lower quote when we first started working, it was a huge deal for her to put me in something else she was producing where she had the power to raise my quote, even doubling it. (Nowadays they can't do that. Your quotes are private and unable to be used to match other projects because it can hold your salary back, which is why what Queen did back then was such a Boss-Ass Move.) And this was all based on the relationship I built with her.

So I think there's so much room for perspective in these conversations that people may not be considering. It's really not always black-and-white. There are so many layers to how decisions are made and I'm someone who's learned how to take all those different things into consideration. It shouldn't solely be about the money. It should also be about the experience and your proximity to being associated or affiliated with said project, individual, or company (that you respect, of course). Like, I'll be the first to admit that I'll go running to Disney whenever they call. And not because of the money solely, but because I like the work that they do. Their work is well-thought-out and it's inspiring. It's Disney!

I feel the same way with Broadway, which is why I'm so excited to be working with Debbie Allen on a new show. Broadway's not paying me too much, but let's be real, Broadway don't pay nobody that much. But guess what? I'm gonna be playing Muhammad Ali's first wife, Sonji Roi, who represents a lot of things that I value in life. And I love Broadway because it's one of the only jobs outside television that you can have real consistency with as an actor. Movies have a start and finish; it's quick. There's usually a longer time spent rehearsing when you're part of a Broadway show, so now I have a consistent schedule that works for me. And I can spend more time with my son while working with the fabulous Debbie Allen, who I've always wanted to work with. I'm gonna be in New York City, and I *love* New York because that's where I found myself. I've been on the West Coast for most of the year, which I love in its own way, but the change in scenery can only do wonders for my spirit and ever-changing character! There is a whole other side of me that exists on the East Coast, and so many other careers I get to explore. So spending time with me, my family, performing an entirely new role, and learning from Debbie Allen? Sounds good to me!

I don't want to lie to y'all. I don't want to lie to anybody, period. I want to tell y'all the truth, because I want all of us to get to a place to take action based on what we know. When people talk about knowledge and power, it's the lack of this knowledge that actually makes people powerless. It's them not actually knowing the truth of how things work. In my opinion, there's danger, a lot of times, when people just go out there and complain and state these problems without guiding you to some potential solutions. They don't tell you how to get around it or how to empower yourself. And water only runs from the tap in one direction. So are you gonna move your cup in the direction that it's going, or are you gonna try to force it to move in the opposite direction when it wasn't meant to? I promise you, you're gonna get tired! And you deserve better than pure exhaustion.

So here I am, telling you all the ways to consider looking at your glass half-full, making sure y'all know you can empower yourselves with a bit of perspective, and sharing some of these harsh truths that can propel you forward both professionally and personally. Don't drag me through the mud, now.

8

THE POWER OF PARENTHOOD

When I think about motherhood, I think about the power it brought me. From carrying the baby, to the roller coaster of emotions, to pushing the baby out with no epidural—yeah, I'm lying—how could I not think about the strength that persevered during that time?

    I loved being pregnant! At the same time, pregnancy was hard for me emotionally. Everyone was so excited, but I felt like I was dealing with a lot of people and their different emotions—my son's father included—and I felt really sensitive and irritated (which I kind of often am already, so yikes). It was strange, and also uncomfortable because I felt like everything was too real. Maybe that's a testament to the hormone imbalance and the psychology a person goes through with being pregnant, but for some reason I didn't know if I was overreacting in certain situations or not. At the same time, I was going on tour for *Nope* and I was also on the international tour for *Lightyear*. So I was very much in the public eye regardless of if I felt really ugly and not cute, which was so stressful on my relationship at the time.

But then I also felt like my son was working his magic inside me, kicking me with his tiny feet, as if to say, *Mom, we good. Don't worry about nothing.* The emotional connection was so immediate and intimate. Being pregnant was giving me a different kind of security and strength, one that reminded me I was never really alone. You really can't get closer to anybody in the world. Like, we *can* have other people inside us, if you know what I mean, but it ain't like that, you know?

When I was younger, it was harder to find the line of boundaries between myself and others. My accolades have always come from self-sacrifice, and I can talk about it all day, every day. But after having my son, all that changed. My son needed me—and not only did he need me to be okay emotionally as a provider, but he also needed me as his main food source. Even at the most primal level, he needed me to nourish him. And even if I didn't breastfeed, I had a responsibility to provide him with whatever he needed! That changed me and my ability to distinguish what I needed—the things that were equal to my sacrifices—and the things I did not.

Before having a kid, I was having such a hard time saying no to people. Having my son made me feel like, *Bitch, you better figure it the fuck out because he needs you most.* It made me love myself more than ever so that I could be great for him. That shift has made me extraordinarily powerful because now I'm just pouring into myself more than ever before. I'm understanding how to continuously build my self-worth because I know that he's watching me now. I want him to be able to learn by watching the best of me and being proud of me when I pull through at my worst. I've done things in the past that really didn't serve me. I had to sacrifice my discomfort in saying no to show up in the best way for my son, and that has given me really great power.

At the same time, sometimes it's hard to choose yourself, but I do because I know if I don't, I'm not the best version of myself. I can't be the best mom. So, in reality, it's all about him again, but the love is so magical because what he pushes me to be helps both him and me. We are constantly watering each other's wells with love and growth. Last year I had to turn down hosting the Oscars red carpet (but shout-out to my girl Vanessa Hudgens; she ate down), and as a certified workhorse, that was difficult. But I'm not doing anything that takes me away from being able to be 100 percent for my son.

Like, Son, you are really the light of my life even though you really, really don't like it when I kiss you. My heart.

Over the years, I've reflected on my own parents' journey, the things they sacrificed in order to get to where we all are now. The older I got, the more I understood their emotional truths.

Once my mother confessed, "You know, I was scared as hell when we went to Montreal for you to shoot *The Wool Cap* when you were ten years old. It was your first leading role, but I had to go without your dad and be out there with you alone."

Really? I thought.

She continued. "I had to go out there and be with you, but I would look at you and I would say, 'Well, if she can do it, I can do it, too.'"

It was such a real and major moment because I really didn't see any of that in my mom. I mean, I knew she would say, "You are making my nerves bad," but I had no idea how intense it was for her or that I was her source of power. My mom let go of her sense of fear, her worries, her anxieties, all because she saw me paving the road ahead of me and had my back. I was fortunate that my parents were aware of the generational struggles and the cycles of depression and apathy that could've consumed our family. To take a risk and uproot our lives for the sake of cultivating the space of opportunity, even through all the uncertainty of being an entertainer, is the power of parenthood.

That said, I do know a lot of people who are missing out on this powerful connection because they've judged their parents' actions so heavily that they end up not having any compassion for them. Forgiveness doesn't mean reconciliation, but for your own personal growth and for your own personal power, you have to be able to break down their narrative and not hold your parents in a negative light because, you might not realize it but, it can put a strain on you and your outlook on life, too. It took me a long time to even see my parents as regular people.

I went through this phase where I was being a bad, judgmental teen. Not that I was ashamed about where they came from, but I was always reminded in subtle ways about their background. My dad's from Cabrini-Green, which used to be a project in Chicago, and my mom grew up in Robbins, which was a more rural part of Illinois. You know, they were never what I call "fancy people," which at the time I would use against them, but I had to understand that this is just who they are! And even to this day, they're not materialistic people (which makes holidays very easy).

I was always conflicted when I went to work. In this space, with every movie I would go on, I was doing different things and learning different things from my siblings. I was just being exposed to stuff that they were not being exposed to, but it was their sacrifices, both external and internal, that allowed me to have the exposure. There was a period when I kept telling myself, *I'm better than this. They don't get me. They don't understand.*

We all do this. We don't realize that we are who we are because of our parents' sacrifices. And it's important that we look at those aspects of ourselves that we got from our parents that are positive because then we're able to lean deeper into what our power is. If you denounce the power that you have by denouncing your parents, you are also disempowering yourself in a lot of ways. I gained a lot of my personal power by forgiving my parents and loving them and appreciating them for who they were and who they were not.

And I needed these critical, bitter thoughts to understand that who I am is who my parents would've been had they had these resources. If my parents had the opportunities to do what I'm doing, if my parents had someone telling them to believe in themselves, if my parents had somebody that encouraged them like they did to me—they would be me. I'm an extension of their wildest dreams.

It's really awesome that my parents created a safe space for us to heal. I'll be honest, I do think that because of what I learned, because of what they exposed me to with therapy and all that type of stuff, I became the difficult younger millennial pushing them to see the error of their ways. Or I'd show them the mess I'd have to clean up in my life because of them, rawr. The typical young adult journey where you realize you have to grow up and stop being mad that you weren't raised perfectly. While that's necessary for a young adult to accept, it's equally important that a parent can take a little justified Yelp review. I'm grateful that my parents were open to hearing my perspective.

Still my experiences were so unique in that I gained a lot of knowledge so young because I had an inordinate amount of access. Sometimes I would speak as if I had all the keys to the kingdom, saying things like, "Look where I am because I'm twenty-one. Maybe I have something to offer to you guys. Maybe what I'm saying is of value. Now I'm not a kid anymore. I'm saying this to you as an adult. And I'm still living my purpose and doing my thing. So listen to me!"

And they did. But they were also there when I realized it wasn't as easy to use wisdom in an experience it's necessary for. That's what I had to learn. That's what caught up to me. I thought I had so much wisdom as a kid and there were a lot of the things that I thought and felt like they were true, but they were proven through my experience. And through that experience, I came back around to understanding and realizing that I always knew. But I needed those experiences to help me understand what it means to go through something, in order to articulate it that way.

During a conversation I had with two friends, I was talking about my relationship with my parents. How I had to kind of shrink in many ways and about how they often would respond to me out of fear. There would be scenarios where I would warn them about someone—an agent or a manager—and what I said would become true. Or I would say, "Hey, we should do this thing because I think it'll pay off." And it would! There would just be many times when I challenged them not listening to their inner voice and instead taking things at face value, and I would call out anything that felt inauthentic. All this was good for me, but what ended up happening was that it freaked my parents out. In no way was I smarter than them, because obviously I didn't have the experience, but I was smarter and intuitive in a way even I could not explain. So it caused a rift in our parent-child dynamic. Sometimes, they would treat me in a way that was stifling, that would make me feel powerless, like I could not share that inner knowing that made me me. I would lose myself and have to self-abandon for the sake of surviving in my household. In other words, I had to "stay in a child's place." Through my experience with them, my wisdom was then vindicated. I knew what I just explained to you as a kid but I didn't have the years of adversity to truly own my power in the way I do now. While it hurt that my parents did not embrace me in those moments, it created the space for me to embrace myself. Because just like I hadn't had an experience that made me not trust myself yet, that's all my parents had. Through their shortcomings they were still pushing and supporting me, putting me in places where I could be seen and encouraged, and that's why I did trust my inner voice, even though they had years of people crushing theirs. We are all special and we all already know it; it's just about finding our way back.

The wisdom was always there; I always trusted myself, but here I was put into a situation where all I had was myself to trust. Now I don't just believe it to be true, I *know* it to be true. Now I really see myself and own myself. I have the awareness to back up what I'm saying. I have the awareness, the experience, and the clarity of why what I was saying and why what I brought to the table influenced my value and my perspective and my inner knowing of myself. And to repeat, the greatest part of all this was that through my learning and my self-awareness, my parents were participants. They granted me the access and met me where I was.

There's the fear that comes into people trying to control how you wield power, which is what I was dealing with in my own household. When my parents saw that I was stepping into my power, and they saw that I knew I was powerful, they were like, *Oh no, we don't want this for her.* They were scared that I was going to abuse my power and, honestly, they almost crushed me just a bit. Just a tinge. But they just wanted to make sure that I didn't become somebody who leveraged it over others, which, looking back, I can understand now.

In a way, my parents have always kept me grounded. Because my family was never materialistic, I've always been aware that my greatest resources are the people around me and the love and the relationships that I have in my life. I've always been told that real wealth is something that's already inside me and, eventually, it will attract wealth in the material sense.

To be cash rich, to be asset rich, to be relationships rich, ask yourself, which one is the greater value? If you ask me, I love an asset or two, and I love having cash in my account. But if I'm relationship rich? If I'm rich in my resources, and the people who I know love me and genuinely care about me? Baby, I'm never gonna go broke.

9
UNDERSTAND YOUR SELF-WORTH

My forgiveness and faith always seemed to be intertwined. Because I grew up Catholic, I think it's fair to say that Christians of any denomination often struggle with personal boundaries. I was raised with the idea that all could be forgiven. The concept of unconditional love and forgiveness runs so deep because I'm focused on my walk with God. I spent so much time trying to love people through their toughest circumstances because I truly do not judge and that's intense. Preachers or deacons, including my father, would go into prisons and pray with people who've committed the most heinous crimes.

You might think, *Why? That person doesn't deserve it.* And they may not. But they don't deserve it not because they are not worthy, but because they don't believe they are. We have to realize that we are all worthy by birthright and this is beyond what we might believe religiously. Just because we are worthy doesn't mean we will walk that righteous walk—and that's the danger. Even still, I found myself in so many situations misinterpreting that my perception of someone's goodness doesn't necessarily mean they want to *be* good. Sometimes they're actually a certified asshole.

Through my Biblical teachings, I heard messages that were similar to "accept bullshit from people because in the end they will realize their worth and be better" and that's one of the main things displayed in Jesus's story when He is denied by Peter. Don't misinterpret my words—I'm not here to be God or Jesus. I'm actually here to praise Him as I walk my walk and realize how difficult it is to make the choices He made and understand that what He represents stands as an inspiration for what I can and will overcome. Not necessarily what I should take or endure because He's already endured it for me. But worthiness sometimes gets muddled in our humble interpretations of parables.

My worth was built on service, because that's how my family was. That was what my religion was: service and self-sacrifice even to the point of self-abandonment. And this isn't a critique on the church or the Bible, but a critique on myself and my interpretation.

All my value at a young age, even before performing and then reinforced through performing, was about using what I had to make other people happy and feel good about themselves. To be a clown, a court jester. To show that I cared, even if it made me bleed, so that someone else could feel important. I ignored my feelings when people hurt me so that they didn't feel bad. I never felt insecure, I always loved myself, but my actions said I loved others more than me. Simply because I thought that was what Jesus would do, but in turn it created a scenario of my own low self-worth. Self-worth as defined by helping others when we are only truly capable of helping and saving ourselves is a road to misery. That doesn't mean you can't be of service; that doesn't mean you can't love and help out, but if your self-worth is *built* on saving others, you're setting yourself up for failure taking on a job only His love can handle.

I am still learning what self-worth means to me and breaking the idea that self-worth is something you just naturally have. Because you don't just have it, actually. We all have to work extra hard to build our self-worth through different circumstances for our entire lives because it's been tainted by others from the very beginning. By our family, friends, and our circumstances. By many things that are based on proximity but are also based on things out of our control. Then we create habits based on that, and then people judge us as adults as if we're already supposed to know something we otherwise would not have known because it hadn't been taught to us.

We must take on the task of being the most important thing in our lives, because if we don't, we are no good to anyone. So, regardless of if it's your job, your friend, your partner, that coworker, *whatever*, if it's solely depleting you and not giving you the energy in return, you need to go on and be better. You must let it go. The checks and balances of how you feel about the people and things in your life are an important exchange of give and take. If it just feels like taking, and you don't feel nourished in all your encounters to some degree, that means a boundary should be placed because it's creating an imbalance in your ability to maintain.

In what I consider "the Catholic guilt," I do think we take on this burden of being the holy ones and put this intense pressure on ourselves to continuously forgive people, flaws and all. But in reality, it's hard to live by that because sometimes people do hurt you. I had to learn that everybody is not capable of embracing love. Whether you are reading this as a believer or a nonbeliever, which is your choice, the facts still stand. No matter what we do, or who we are, people have to decide who they want to be. They may be beautiful people who face the sun every morning, but then when the sun does go down, they bask in the shadows and try to pull you in, too.

And the biggest piece of this is letting yourself know it's okay if you do not want to walk in the shadows with those you care for anymore. For your own survival, you could either break away or be present while they come to terms with their own growth. Again, this is easier said than done, trust me. It hurts to see someone stuck in a cycle of bad habits and of course, they can do it *and* of course, they've been through a lot, and, and, *and!* You can justify their actions for the rest of eternity, but it won't matter! Judas could've been forgiven but he could not forgive himself and that's the reality for many people who can't turn the page on their own transgressions. The truth is their suffering isn't your own, so don't make it your own. Their guilt isn't yours to bear and you cannot alleviate their journey. You can't fix people's problems for them, so stop trying to fix shit! A job like that is too supreme for another human being to manage. A person's change and accountability truly have to come from within. I'm speaking to you, and talking to me, too!

(I like to remember that the enemy can do their worst if it means you've done your best. All the enemy has is your fear, your shame, your feelings of unworthiness, and your ignorance to think you can fix what only God can. Lay it all unto Him, because once you see he cannot hurt you, love, you will be free!)

This year, as I continued stepping into my own power, I had to come to terms with my survivor's remorse. Sometimes we think of survivor's remorse solely as someone living and another becoming unalive. However, it is, to me, much more than that. Everyone in life experiences trauma. All of us. There are some of us who survive and there are some of us who mentally become blocked. It's not easy. Our bodies have moved on, but our minds are still there. When you're a person who can move on mentally, you are a survivor in life. The remorse can be so dangerous because when you see kindred spirits, or you just see others in life who can't get past their mental blocks, then you may feel it's your job to pull them up. While it's sad realizing you have to leave people behind, it's beautiful to finally let go of the burden that makes you think you can't. It's also then your responsibility to stay risen because when your parents first teach you how to walk, they don't crawl beside you. They actively walk alongside you until you learn to stand up and do it yourself. Watching amazing people self-destruct is hard, but people can only save themselves. I want to tell you I don't know why you survived and they didn't, but I can tell you that because you have, you will inspire a lot of people.

Figuring all this out was really important for my own boundaries, not with others but with myself. I would look at others and see a version of myself that was hurting and would relive the trauma with them even though I got past it, hoping and thinking it would help them through. In reality it was just emotionally draining me and stopping this person from doing their own personal work, which is what it takes. I believe love should have conditions because I believe there is already an unconditional force that loves us all. We aren't here to do that; we are here to experience being human, and that includes happiness and pain. Because in that pain we turn inwards, where the truest love will always be.

10

POWER DYNAMICS

Don't get me wrong, stepping into your power will always come with backlash. There's always going to be someone who's thinking, *Man, why can't you just be grateful for the experience and shut up?* I've experienced so many negative and cruel responses when I decided enough was enough on many occasions.

I remember a few years ago when I spoke up about my experience with an R&B singer who I'd once considered a friend. Everyone and their mama accused me of lying and trying to take this man down. I was getting dragged anywhere I had a following. Even worse, they thought I was trying to get attention when in reality I was only trying to stand up for myself when I didn't want to be part of his music video. He pressured me endlessly about it at a kickback that I definitely didn't expect to be working at, and he tried to kiss me, as if that would make me feel important or special. I had to physically push him off. Then, when he filmed a piece of me on the couch and showed it to me, as if I would oblige, I still said no! I tried so hard in the moment to do what I thought I should, which essentially meant that I would be sacrificing my comfort for his.

Honestly, I didn't want him to be offended; I didn't want my anxiety and fear to make him feel guilty. I had also been drinking and simply wasn't sure if I was overreacting or not. I felt so bad that instead of leaving, I hid in a nearby closet out of fear that if I left it would make him feel a type of way towards me. When he found me in the closet and told me I didn't need to do what he'd wanted, he assured me I didn't have to be in the video. So, I didn't have to be afraid. I went home thinking the worst was over.

Of course, folks be lying. The video came out with me in it, and I felt so disrespected and unheard, I couldn't even hide my disappointment. I was capital-*T* Tired. I had already swallowed my feelings in the process of that pressure cooker situation. I'd been cool about everything; the very least he could've done was leave my ass out of the damn video. So I went off! I raised my voice. I made it public, and I stood up for myself when I called him out on his behavior.

People really did hate me for it. How dare someone like me speak out against their celebrity crush? He was an attractive man. He was seen as such a sex symbol that in their minds, they didn't think someone like him would need to harass and intimidate a woman to get what he wanted. In reality, it was never about him liking me or not; it was about power. Someone like him believes his sexual prowess is his power. It wasn't that he *wanted* me; it was the idea that he thought I wanted him and that in my wanting him, he could get me to be in the video. In simple terms: it was actually plain, old, regular-degular sexual harassment.

And even though he was someone I admired in a platonic, almost familial way, in that moment—and even sometimes to this day—I'm seen as a target from both his fans and from people who simply don't like when a woman speaks out about things that make people uncomfortable. It's uncomfortable to impose a boundary in private, so imagine how uncomfortable it is when it feels like it was forced to happen in public, too?

It's also uncomfortable for those involved and for those watching because it impacts the status quo and how people may or may not come forward about certain situations. It also impacts the framework of how people decide what's okay to bring to the table. Before then, this was someone who was creating these harmful spaces for a lot of girls, and I don't know if young women felt empowered to mention it. It's so embedded in the industry and in life. Rape culture, in general, is too normalized, and because of the power dynamics, the male ego is at the forefront of what we all must pacify. Any woman speaking out becomes a threat to those who are benefiting from that and the women who are afraid to rock that boat.

For me, it wasn't about him. I don't hate that man. Honestly, I'd still listen to one of the two hits he has, he doesn't own the masters anyway. It was truly about the principle and the growing respect and esteem I had for myself. It was about me making sure everyone knew I was coming into my own as a whistleblowing-ass bitch. It was a warning: if you do something improper to me, I will put yo ass on notice! I made my decision that I didn't want to be fucked with ever again. And maybe I didn't do what I felt I should in the moment because I was scared, but I grew enough from that moment to know that I would be better to myself the second time around.

As an entertainer, people often feel like they're entitled to every detail of your life. But in all honesty would you go to your day job and start talking about the fight you had with your partner over dinner the night before? Or, moreover, would you feel they were entitled to know what happened in your home? Whose business is it but you and yours?

I wish sealed documents could stay sealed, but as a public figure it seems nothing is private. I don't wish to paint a negative image of anyone, especially someone who's half of someone who's so special to me. Life sometimes doesn't go as planned, and sometimes you have to make tough decisions, and that's okay. It's better to leave a situation than to try to force someone into being what you want. I saw the red flags early on, but I focused on the green. And I thought that was the point—not to find someone perfect but someone to grow with.

I was in a relationship, a genuine relationship, with someone, and it just turned into something unhealthy. The relationship was no longer bringing out the best in either of us. I wish I could say he was terrible the entire time or that I was (I'm perfect so that couldn't be the case, obvi) but it wasn't that black-and-white, and that was the problem. I can't explain why it went the way it did, but what I do know is that one of us had to put an end to it existing as it was, or there could've been a big mistake that would've irreversibly affected both of our lives.

I didn't want my son to grow up watching people poorly manage their emotions. I didn't want my son to grow up believing that relationships worked in extremes. I didn't want my son to grow up in an unhappy, unhealthy household. I want my son to see and know love from two people who see each other as equals and are mature enough to think as a unit, because that's what I saw growing up. The house is no good when it's made of glass. He deserves better and I will always fight for him to have this level of normalcy.

We ruin such beautiful people by not holding them accountable. We are all perfect on our own, it's only when we get into relationships or even close friendships that things become difficult. We have to communicate more, balance our emotions, learn boundaries—and not just the other person's boundaries, but our boundaries with that person. I personally think it takes a lot of maturity. When I was younger, I remember my parents saying, "You aren't ready for a boyfriend." Shit, I'm thirty-one and still not sure if I'm ready! I damn sure know these thirty-one-year-old men ain't ready. Yes, I said it! Most of them don't know their own emotions exist, let alone know how to express them to someone else. Not to mention, patriarchy tells men they are perfect and that they're leaders without giving them the responsibility of being accountable for when they fall short. And though I don't truly believe in gender rules, if a man *is* hot to wear the pants, I need to see some true leadership qualities. And no, not just having money like people love to say online. Because having money doesn't mean you a) have a plan for us, b) communicate effectively, or c) have patience and the ability to defuse. To be a leader is to be an example. You can't be out here acting crazy but then wanting someone to take notes, 'cause if you're acting crazy and I'm following you, then now I'm acting crazy, too! That's just not going to work. When we see these qualities in others (and ourselves), we do everyone a disservice by not holding them (and ourselves) accountable for these actions.

I do urge anyone out there who has dealt or is dealing with this kind of dynamic to understand that walking away is the only way to obtain resolution. Someone who has a raging cough, a stuffy nose, and chills can't get better if they themselves can't look in the mirror and acknowledge that they're unwell. And if you are with someone who is apparently unwell, you must know you're unwell, too, because why else do you relate? It's not about blaming ourselves for the situations we find ourselves in, but it is about understanding how we got there.

People are good, but do they want to *be* good and is that good good enough for you? Moreover, is their good even your version of good? Like when we date people, it's important to see them for who they are, the parts we like and the parts we don't. The glimpses that we get of the parts we see our future selves with genuinely do exist within that person, but do those parts align with who they want to be?

This, to me, is the choice of love and its roots in identity. The act of suiting up and doing what it takes to create a space for the love you want with someone else to last can impact your direction in life. It takes awareness, intention, and compromise on both ends. It's something I realized through this experience that made me redefine what is important in my life. I've asked myself: What does a relationship truly take to call someone a life partner, what does it mean for your individuality? And how do we respond or deal with that being challenged by a *we* instead of a *me*? Deciding to be solo is a lifestyle choice, but props to those in long-term relationships, because to think as a unit, to create a safe space for someone and to trust them to do it for you... wow. It takes the right partner, yes, but also a particular mindset. Respect.

I'm not angry with my son's father anymore. I love him so much as a human being even though things will never be the same, but maybe that's the point. I chose him to be the father of my son. I know he is a great person, but does that mean we are great for each other? I don't know. And accepting that was a hard step for both of us.

I don't regret the journey we took to get there because I learned some important lessons and my son is the best parts of both of us, and boy is that a perfect combination. Coparenting is not a competition; it's not a battle of who will take care of our son better. It's about our son. And my son's idea of self-worth begins with his father and me.

The fallout of our relationship, especially through the court system, was the hardest thing I ever had to go through. But I knew no other way to bring order to the situation for both of us because it had truly gotten above me. I didn't want people to hate him or think he was crazy and judge his entire character on the worst aspects that I experienced. But, most importantly, I didn't want my son to think his father is a monster, because I don't. And if I am a trigger for someone else, the best thing I could do was to remove myself before all was destroyed.

I ended the cycle the best way I knew how. And the focus for me will always be about working as a team with this person in the best role we will ever play: loving parents to Leo! Neither of us will be perfect, but if anyone could make us put on our best performance to achieve this goal, it would be our son. And my hope is that as my son builds his own self-worth, he can begin by watching us think enough of ourselves to be better.

11

FOR MY ENTREPRENEUR BADDIES

Quick intermission for all of you reading this book, and all of you looking to level up! Listen, you know you can become an asset to any business you collaborate with if you are ambitious; if you know the difference between an LLC and a corporation; if your stock portfolio is spread through international markets; if you ain't got no car note 'cause ya car paid owfff; if you know to lease a car instead of buying it; if you need a business manager because you actually have business to manage; if you know to invest your money in real estate; if your real estate isn't even in your name, but a trustee's; if you only spend money to make money; if the IRS can hit your pockets for six or seven figures; if you got a house anywhere in Texas 'cause... well, you know; if you got a Square account; if you got your own shit; if you stay in your own lane and get to yo moneyyyy; if you pray for your haters; if you pray for your family; if you pray over your dreams; if you are a leader; if you are a believer; if you, in the words of Beyoncé, can upgradeeee a mf baby.

If you can or do any, or all, of these things, *you* are an asset!

It's not giving liability; it's giving *I'm the asset who got assets WITH the assets, okay?*

It's giving wordplay; it's giving double entendre. This one is for my entrepreneurial baddies who want to shake shit up.

I wrote this song called "Assets" and obviously it's a play on physicality as well as a play on mentality, even more so than just your actual finances. Financial literacy is obviously important to me as someone who has had to have business managers since I was twelve because my parents didn't know how to teach me to manage such large sums of money. By the grace of God they did know what direction to point me in to find that help. The ability to understand how to manage my finances empowers me a lot. It's not just the amount of money I make but how I use it, and that's a skill. If you have a million dollars but don't know how to manage it, it's pointless. A person with $500 could create a better cyclical chain of cash flow even if they have started with much less. That, to me, is what it means to be an asset. To understand what to do with what you got. If you got it, flaunt it, you know? Know your power!

I have faith, and to me that's an asset. My ability to love and be loved, that's an asset. The way you live when you think in abundance—to me, those are the assets we need more to survive in life. I had fun with the "Assets" video; it's one of my favorites I ever did. It's like a mini movie with a few different characters;

I do a nod to *Coming to America* and Whoopi Goldberg in *Ghost*. Overall, with my art, the greatest story within the stories I tell is autonomy, ownership, and entrepreneurialism. One being one's own business—that's how we must think now to even have a chance at moving through this corporate space. To see ourselves as a corporation, which, in business as a child actor, is one of the first things they tell you to do. Corporatize yourself, because you are a business.

12

A WEIRD, RANDOM MOMENT FROM SET

I remember there was a time when I was on a set and, honey, the girls were fighting. Let me set the scene. We were running through lines. The script used vitriolic language, and the actress, let's call her Brenda, was saying her lines to another actress, let's call her Barbara, who seemed to be getting to her. "Cunt!" Brenda would yell each time, getting more and more aggressive with it. And instead of Barbara saying her lines, she'd grow flustered, etc.

It was hilarious (A LITTLE), but it was also upsetting Barbara and making our shoot days longer. I gotta be honest. I thought it was white folks' shit; like, who really cares that Brenda's crazy ass was being a lil method with her bully role, she ain't nobody! But it was becoming a consistent issue every other day. I felt bad that Barbara was taking it personally, and I really wanted to go home, because them days were long.

So one day it gets to a head and Barbara is crying in my trailer again and saying she's going to call HR, because it was a whole debacle. Like the de-escalator I try to be in most friendships, I decided to intervene.

"Let's be chill! Let's all have fun and respect each other—"

It was then that Brenda cut me off. "Keke, literally, just don't. Who do you think you are? Martin Fucking Luther King?"

At the time, all I could think was, *I'm the one with my foot in your ass*, juuuust kidding. I kept my cool. "Really, Brenda?"

The point is I knew the type of person Brenda was. I *know* who she is. And her comment doesn't bother me because she wasn't someone I cared about, respectfully, and I was getting paid for my time whether she called me Malcolm, Martin, Shirley, Mother Nature—whoever!

Brenda tried to diminish me in a way I'm not even sure she had the awareness to realize. I think her self-absorption and entitlement are so ingrained that she is just repeating what it means to get whatever she wants without consequence. To shut me down or attempt to shut me down by comparing me to a world leader who was assassinated for spreading peace was beyond tone-deaf. But she wanted me to care and I wish I could tell you guys I did but I didn't because she was never important to me. She was important to Barbara and that set but not to Keke Palmer. I knew exactly what that was and I would never allow my energy to be wasted explaining my worth to someone who doesn't even know their worth outside what society has told them it should be. If I got paid every time an ignorant white person said something that bothered me, I would be retired, lounging on several stacks of Benjamin Franklins in Saint-Tropez. My parents raised me in Illinois, and it's still very racist (despite how much Jussie might've thrown some of y'all off). And maybe my parents did raise me with some of Martin's values, even though both Malcolm and Martin were actually more similar than we were ever taught in school. Martin's choice to stand in his power and peace by choosing not to be affected by the noise is what I had to learn as my way of life, too. As a woman, I can't just let everything a misogynist says bother me. It's so important not to get caught up in other people's drama, because sometimes that's all they want you to do. That was their shit, not my shit, and even in stepping in and helping out, I would still not let it become my shit.

I know who I am is what I'm saying. And it's okay that some people won't accept that, or that they will antagonize me about the core elements of my identity. Some of them will be white and, shit, some of them will be Black. It's a distraction more than anything.

Be safe out there.

13
THE DARKNESS WILL ACTUALLY HELP YOU

There's this misconception about darkness always being the worst and ugliest moments of your life. And I'm here to tell you something you probably don't want to hear: the best things are brewing during your darkest hours. How you make it through the darkness will inform your purpose, and I encourage you to embrace it. I had to learn to reframe my aversion to darkness because it helped me find grace with myself during the most challenging years of my life. I'm not saying it's easy, but I'm saying that you can become a better version of yourself for you and others around you.

Physics proves that you can only go so far before something good comes back. I'm no physicist, but my understanding is that there is only so far you can go in one direction before you must go in the other. This is why ups and downs are constants in life. The circumstances are binary, but we can be the nuance in between. It's our amazing ability as conscious beings. And for a Christian, my concept of faith is that I won't be put through anything that I can't handle, or I won't be put through anything that isn't meant to transform me. My come-to-Jesus moment with myself when things become difficult is simply: *There's no way this can last.*

In the moments when you're deep in it? The darkness sucks. It always feels like the worst thing that's happening in my life, like I'm playing defense, but the offense is constantly in the paint, shooting layups (I hope I said that right). I tell myself that I don't want to go through this and that it's the last thing I wanna endure. But I remind myself that it can only be so bad before everything goes back to normal again. And so I just try to tell myself to have patience and to pay attention to the journey that I'm on. I walk along the path I'm meant to learn from. The biggest downside for me when I'm going through a difficult time would be to not be present enough in the experience to learn what I have to learn so I don't have to go through it again.

I like to ask myself, *Why did this happen for me? What am I supposed to learn?* And I encourage you to ask yourself these same questions. Because there is a reason why I'm facing certain challenges, there is a reason why this *thing* is happening. And even if this is some tired tale that humans tell themselves while they go through this existential crisis of existence, I'm still gonna say there is a reason. Even if it's all for nothing. Because at that point, I might as well make it fun for myself and create the reason and just treat it like a lesson, as if I'm at school. Like if I have to be here, I might as well learn something from this discomfort, otherwise I'm actively making *sure* it's pointless.

You should think of your moments of darkness like exams. You go to school, learn some new things, and then take an exam based on what you've learned. And I don't know about you, but exams can be really, really fucking hard for me. It doesn't matter if I'm giving short written responses or filling in multiple-choice answers on a Scantron; being tested about what I should know always stimulates a kernel of self-doubt, even when I'm the smartest person in the class.

But in my case, I try to do the work of paying as much attention as I possibly can in the classroom. And boy did I hate the geometry and biology lessons. I hated the fuck out of everything so much, but I knew I had to pay attention. I have to. Because when it's time for the exam, I want to pass. I need to pass in order to get to the next thing and advance in the area of my personal development and wellness. With a career in entertainment, I don't think I really needed biology, but I do need the discipline of following through on the most difficult tasks in order to get past them. And so that's how I've shifted my outlook on hard times. I know I don't want to do it, I don't want to be there, but this is happening for some reason outside my control. And how much I was paying attention to the lessons in the classroom was going to factor into how I moved through the exam to get to the other side. (I just had to make sure I wasn't trying to avoid or reschedule the exam, especially if that level of confrontation was too hard for me. Because even if I didn't deal with it then, I'd have to eventually.)

And I don't mean just getting to a place where I was no longer in it, but really challenging myself to thrive simultaneously. What I mean by that is a lot of times we rush past things. The concept of surviving to me doesn't just mean you made it out of the wilderness. Going through hard times doesn't just include making it out, it includes who you become when you do. How that event changed you or made you evolve as a person while making sure you're just as proud of the person you were before. And that is sometimes more difficult than just living through the incident. As people, we're pretty adamant about wanting a traumatic event to be over, because we want to be on the other side of it. But I'm convinced it's bigger than that. Thriving is not just surviving the traumatic event, but living in the "new you" that was created through the experience with pride. You have the ability to become the greatest version of yourself, even if that means losing whatever (or whoever) in the process of becoming anew.

I don't want to play it safe, and no one who is around me and says they love me should want me to play it safe! Because through me people see the possibilities. Me being brave allows others to be brave, and that allows the next person to also be brave. Everything you've been through is so you can create better boundaries, be bolder, and have experiences that validate your wisdom and choices. To self-abandon is to understand the value of self-protection! This is something I learned through my experience and self-work with therapy. It was truly profound to me when my therapist brought me to the realization that I get closer to my authenticity by going through experiences that force me to stand up for myself. Standing up for myself creates boundaries, and it constantly evolves my sense of self.

Everything is for you to be reminded that you are more than capable of rising to the occasion. Your authenticity is birthed through trials and tribulations and your winning is not only through surviving but thriving! On a soul level, you should want this for you. Because you deserve it.

Don't get caught up in the performance of human life, because you know on a soul level that you are greater than your circumstances. But it is the journey of being challenged in which we continue to show ourselves we are worth choosing. We have to go to school to graduate. And no, this isn't a Freudian slip. It's a Freudian on purpose. Keep going!

All these experiences are not in vain. At the end of the day, you gotta think about the things that make you you. No one can ever be you, because they have never lived your life or stepped in your shoes. No one can ever tell your story because you have to tell that story. It's all part of your process. It's all part of using those unique pieces of you.

Life is a lot like method acting. I like to think, *We're not these people.* We're a piece of God living a human story and He loves us so much that He created us, just like I created Leo. But He puts us in these circumstances to experience them together. Honestly and truly there is a bittersweet quality to life that you can't really tell someone about. They have to experience it. Remembering that we came from greatness is tough because life will make you forget that. If life is so perfect, you probably think, *What is the meaning?* Great times are great because you have had bad times, but the feeling of getting on the other side of it is only transferred through a shared *human* experience.

And if this is the actual course of life I mean, why *wouldn't* you go through this? I think often about the fact that there's no mistaking that my sister and her kids randomly ended up moving in with me when I was going through a dark period in my life. The purpose of life is to be resilient through it all. We can rise to the occasion of being greater than our circumstances as long as we never stop loving ourselves through it. The level of compassion you show yourself should be as if you'd, like, made it to the final battle with Bowser for the third time. Like, am I gonna beat this weird-looking turtle or do I gotta go to level one all over again? And I'm not gonna judge myself for either of these outcomes, but the ability to live within that is freeing.

Just remember that there are some things that will change you forever. Things that you never thought you'd have to face and that if you did, you would never overcome them. But then you find yourself on the other side and your survival instinct kicks in and propels you through the stratosphere. Before you know it, you aren't the person you were anymore. The person who couldn't survive doesn't exist; they can't exist in you because you survived what they could not. So now here you are with these broken pieces . . . and you're still shining. And you wish that person you were before could fully enjoy who they've become. But there is still this melancholia, this bittersweet taste that you can't get out of your mouth. Because to enjoy it would mean remembering what you had to lose to get there, to shine brighter than any darkness you've been through.

Continue to be a disco ball, shining in certain places while others exist in the shade. I am one, and so are you. Sometimes I cry, but I always smile because I'm so glad I don't look like what I've been through. And I'm glad for everything I went through. I'm such a greater person because of it.

14

I REALLY DO HATE MISOGYNOIR

"How can I hate black women when I date them?"

Very easily, actually; so glad you asked the question! It's very easy to date someone you don't respect when you are looking for ways to feel better about yourself. Even if you are less successful than said woman, there is still a history of propaganda that tells you that you will always be better than she is. This is due to racial oppression and gender oppression. You may think you have created a win-win scenario for yourself to finally be "better" than someone! This is when the one-sided competition begins.

But the gag is, you can't break a spirit that's already been broken *open*. When you experience oppression, at least from where I'm standing, there isn't anything that can take you down. So for my sisters who have found themselves sleeping with an enemy or two...

They were supposed to be able to break you! Everyone said you were an easy target! But you just keep winning and this breaks their reality. They couldn't "beat" the one person that they were supposed to be able to beat, because you weren't competing anyway. And now they're watching you rise up against it all, in the ways they never could. Just know they hate you because you aren't who the world told them you'd be.

Keep winning, y'all; keep creating the only reality there ever was, which is us winning! In love, in work, in life, in *everything*!

I remember writing this because I have experienced jealousy in relationships. Not even jealousy, I would say, 'cause that's too surface. I've experienced envy. People admiring my strength and then getting angry that they cannot emulate it. The patriarchy doesn't even allow them the space to feel it's appropriate to try to learn it through me because I'm a woman. And a Black one at that! I believe, like most marginalized groups, Black women are not what we are said to be. Now, sure, some of us have cultural similarities, but we aren't a monolith and we damn sure do not exist in extension to our oppression. Again, this is how I'm viewing it and how my friend group views it. My awareness of my oppression is there but it does not create apathy in me. So when someone has not experienced a Black woman or has not experienced a Black woman who does not buy into propaganda, that's when all that hate is created out of the admiration and surprise. *Wow, she's amazing and not who I thought she was* quickly turns into *Who does she think she is? She's*

the last person who should be better than me. Insecurities being exposed by someone's power is a dangerous and hard thing. I just wanted to encourage myself and others because culturally, in all our individuality, this is a shared experience. It's really a societal shock that we still stand as tall as we do!

15

AFFIRMATIONS FOR KEKE (AND ANYONE ELSE WHO NEEDS TO HEAR THIS)

HERE'S A REMINDER: KEKE, YOU ARE NOT YOUR PAST MISTAKES. THEY DIDN'T DEFINE YOU THEN AND THEY DON'T DEFINE YOU NOW. YOU WERE YOUNG AND HAD YOUR OWN BATTLES TO OVERCOME. GIVE YOURSELF GRACE AND LET THAT PERSON DEAL WITH THEMSELVES THE WAY THEY SEE FIT BECAUSE IT DOESN'T PERTAIN TO YOU. ALL YOU CAN DO IS WORK ON YOU. DON'T OVE-RIDEALIZE THAT PERSON SIMPLY BECAUSE YOU FEEL BAD ABOUT A PART YOU PLAYED. THAT DOESN'T MAKE THEM BETTER OR WORSE THAN YOU, SO DON'T EVEN FEED INTO THE INFERIORITY CONCEPT OF IT ALL. YOU HAVE FELT BAD, NOTHING CAN CHANGE THAT. YOU DID SOMETHING THAT YOU REGRET AND THAT'S OKAY; YOU

LEARNED SO MUCH. THIS SHOWS THAT YOU ARE IN FACT A GREAT PERSON.

BREATHE AND RELEASE BECAUSE YOU DESERVE SO MUCH GOOD. YOU DESERVE ALL THAT IS ALREADY COMING YOUR WAY.

YOU ARE FOR EVERYBODY. MOREOVER, PEOPLE SEE YOU AS THEY ARE, NOT AS YOU ARE, AND IF THEY DON'T SEE THEMSELVES WELL, CHANCES ARE THEY DON'T SEE YOU WELL, EITHER. NOT TO MENTION, WHO ARE THESE PEOPLE? DO THEY HAVE YOUR RESPECT LIKE THE GOD YOU SERVE? IF THEY DO NOT, THEN THEY SIMPLY DON'T MATTER. WHO ARE THEY TO DEFINE OR CREATE YOUR FUTURE? ONLY YOU AND GOD CAN DO THAT. DO NOT LET THEIR SMALL WAY OF SEEING LIFE BOX YOU IN AND MAKE YOUR WORLD FEEL SMALLER THAN IT IS. REMOVE YOURSELF FROM CHECKING IN WITH DOUBT AND THINKING IT'S GOING TO MAKE YOU BETTER OR THAT YOU'RE GOING TO FIND SOMETHING CONSTRUCTIVE IN IT. NO ONE KNOWS YOU BUT YOU, AND YOU AND GOD HAVE TO DECIDE WHAT EXACTLY IS BEST FOR YOU. WHATEVER THAT IS ... GO AHEAD UNTIL YOU DECIDE OTHERWISE. COMPARISONS DON'T WORK IN THIS CONTEXT BECAUSE YOUR PATH TO HAPPINESS IS SPECIFIC TO

YOU. IT'S NOT DEFINED BY A LIST OF THINGS; IT'S MORE SO YOUR AUTHENTICITY. THAT'S THE ONLY GREAT SUCCESS THAT YOU SHOULD BE AFTER, THE ONE THAT FITS YOU. WALK AWAY FROM ANYTHING THAT DETERS YOU FROM THAT TRUTH.

YOU CAN'T CHANGE WHAT YOU DID YESTERDAY, BUT YOU CAN CHANGE WHAT YOU DO IN THE FUTURE AND APPRECIATE WHAT YOU'VE LEARNED. DWELLING ON WHAT YOU SHOULD'VE, WOULD'VE, OR COULD'VE DONE ONLY ROBS YOU OF THE PRESENT. THERE IS NOTHING TO BE EMBARRASSED ABOUT WHEN FOLLOWING WHAT YOU KNOW AND FOLLOWING YOUR HEART. WHEN UNHAPPY WITH THOSE DECISIONS, MAKE ANOTHER CHOICE THE NEXT TIME. GOD IS WITH YOU.

SO WHAT IF YOU WEREN'T WHO YOU THOUGHT YOU WERE? IT HELPED TURN YOU INTO THE PERSON YOU WANT TO BE, WHICH IS WHO YOU ARE AND WHO YOU'VE ALWAYS BEEN. THESE INSTANCES ONLY TAUGHT YOU WHAT TO LOOK FOR, WHAT TO HIGHLIGHT, AND HOW TO BETTER SUPPORT YOUR PERSONAL WISHES AND MISSION IN THIS LIFE. DON'T CARRY OTHER PEOPLE'S GUILT AND SHAME. LEAVE THAT TO THOSE WHO WERE INVOLVED WHO HAD THEIR OWN LESSONS TO LEARN.

YOU CANNOT BLAME YOURSELF FOR TRUSTING. THAT'S A BEAUTIFUL THING. ALL YOU CAN DO IS BE GRATEFUL THAT YOU LEARNED AND SURVIVED THROUGH GOD'S GRACE. YOU ARE STRONG! YOU SURVIVED AND HAVE SO MUCH MORE TO BE PROUD OF YOURSELF FOR RATHER THAN FEELING ASHAMED.

Self-Doubt Enters.

Sometimes I feel guilty for not being happy. I know I am blessed, and I can see how God has continuously blessed me through each phase of my life. I feel like I have constantly grown and constantly been supported, and things could be so much worse, but they are better than most. It pains me and disappoints me when I allow myself to not focus on that truth.

Self-Doubt Exits.

THIS IS A PART OF THE HUMAN CONDITION. A PART OF COEXISTING IN THIS WORLD. A PART OF YOUR CURIOSITY AND YOUR EMPATHIC NATURE. YOU PICK UP A LOT OF THINGS, BUT YOU ARE LEARNING WHERE TO DROP THEM OFF AND LEAVE THEM. YOU ARE LEARNING NOT TO GO WHERE IT DOESN'T FEEL GOOD, AND THESE FEELINGS ARE A SIGN MORE THAN ANYTHING! A SIGN THAT YOU ARE NOT IN THE PROPER COMPANY, A SIGN THAT YOU NEED TO FIX YOUR PERSPECTIVE, A SIGN OF WHERE

YOU HAVE FALLEN OFF YOUR PRACTICES, A SIGN YOU ARE LETTING THE WRONG THINGS IN YOUR MIND IMPACT YOU. IT'S UP TO YOU TO IDENTIFY WHAT THE TRIGGER IS. DON'T BE AFRAID OF IT. BE HAPPY BECAUSE IT'S TELLING YOU THAT SOMETHING IN YOUR LIFE ISN'T SPEAKING TO YOUR HIGHEST SELF AND IT NEEDS TO BE REMOVED. YOUR SIGNALS ARE WORKING. REMEMBER, THIS IS GOOD.

Believe it or not, I do this internal dialogue a lot where I'll have a conversation with myself like I'm my best girlfriend (because let's be honest, I am). It's a practice that helps me stay in touch with deep emotions that I subconsciously keep even from myself. It also allows me to create kinder thoughts for myself, about myself, because I am creating them in real time by treating myself the way I would a friend. Sometimes we are so unkind to ourselves; that's a bad habit from the brain and all the negative biases out there. Practicing affirmations out loud can help us to unlearn and train our brain to work for us, not against us.

Here is where I encourage you to take a moment to pull out a journal, or a piece of paper of your choosing, and write down how you feel. What worries you? What scares you? How are you honestly feeling about work, friends, love . . . anything?!

When you're done, respond to yourself. Say the things you need to hear, the things you would tell a friend. Remember that your words have power.

MASTER OF ME
SELF-ASSESSMENT EXERCISE

Now that we are at the end of the Power journey, let's chat a little about how to harness some of your individual power!

1. **What is the most important thing to remember when faced with criticism or negativity?**
    a) That my worth is defined by what they think
    b) That I can choose how to see the situation and respond
    c) That I should try better to please them
    d) That I am alone in my struggles

2. **What is the result of comparing yourself to others?**
    a) Increased motivation and inspiration
    b) A clearer sense of my own strengths and weaknesses
    c) A distorted view of my own value and worth
    d) A sense of contentment and satisfaction

3. **What is the key to breaking free from others' projections and expectations?**
    a) Conforming to societal norms and standards
    b) Seeking validation and approval from others
    c) Capitalizing on what makes me different
    d) Ignoring my own needs and desires

4. **What is the key to unlocking your true potential and standing out from others?**
    a) Doing what society does but better
    b) Identifying and amplifying my unique strengths and talents
    c) Comparing myself to others and competing with them
    d) Suppressing my individuality and blending in

(Answers on the next page.)

ANSWER KEY

1. ANSWER: B) THAT I CAN CHOOSE HOW TO SEE THE SITUATION AND RESPOND

REFLECT: How do you currently respond to criticism or negativity, and what would happen if you chose to see the situation differently?

COUNTERACT: When faced with criticism, take a step back, breathe, and remind yourself that objective thinking is key to surviving and thriving. Since opinions are subjective, it's how we reframe them that gives us power—so choose to tell yourself empowering stories, not disempowering ones.

2. ANSWER: C) A DISTORTED VIEW OF MY OWN VALUE AND WORTH

REFLECT: In what ways do you currently compare yourself to others, and how does this impact your self-perception?

COUNTERACT: When you catch yourself comparing yourself to others, redirect the focus to how far you have come. Remind yourself of all the ways that you have grown and will continue to grow. The only comparison should be to who you used to be and how much greater you're becoming.

3. ANSWER: C) CAPITALIZING ON WHAT MAKES ME DIFFERENT

REFLECT: What happens inside you when someone has an expectation of you that doesn't feel quite right? What do you do in that moment?

COUNTERACT: Take time to reflect on your values and strengths, and make intentional choices that align with your authentic self. Be gentle when you make decisions that you realize weren't right for you, because that's how you learn what is.

4. ANSWER: B) IDENTIFYING AND AMPLIFYING MY UNIQUE STRENGTHS AND TALENTS

REFLECT: What's the trait, habit, or aspect of yourself that consistently sparks comments, reactions, or attention from others? What's the part of you that you often find yourself downplaying, hiding, or apologizing for? What would happen if you embraced and amplified that very thing instead of trying to minimize it?

COUNTERACT: Celebrate what makes you stand out simply because it's what separates you. What separates you is what makes you *you* and no one else. This is a good thing. We are often taught to hate ourselves by others who have not learned to love themselves. Love on you! Then you will shine.

OPEN-ENDED QUESTIONS

Pull out your journal and share your thoughts! Here are some more questions that may help you dig a little deeper into your inner power.

- Can you recall a time when someone's opinion or projection made you question your own worth or abilities? How did you respond, and what would you do differently if faced with a similar situation now?
- Have you ever been in a situation where you felt like you had to "prove" yourself to others? What was driving that need, and how did you handle it?
- Have you ever felt like your success or achievements were diminished or dismissed by others? How did you respond, and what did you learn from the experience?
- Think of a moment when you felt like you were being true to yourself, despite external pressures or expectations. What made that possible, and how did it feel?

What drives your sense of self-worth?
    a) My job title and salary
    b) My personal relationships and friendships
    c) My unique strengths and skills
    d) My ability to deliver value to others

REFLECT: What are some ways you've tied your identity to external factors? How can you separate your self-worth from these external measures?

COUNTERACT: The trick here is to focus on how you feel about yourself as a person. Self-esteem and self-worth are constantly growing and they are built on a lot of things. Who we are around, who we say yes to, who we say no to, what we take, etc. It's not one factor but how we choose ourselves in all; simply, choose you.

How do you approach your job?
    a) I give it my all and tie my identity to my work
    b) I do what's required but maintain a healthy work-life balance
    c) I see it as a means to an end and focus on delivering value without emotional attachment
    d) I feel unfulfilled and disconnected from my work

REFLECT: What are some ways you've given away your power to your job? How can you reclaim your agency and autonomy?
COUNTERACT: Approach your job with a sense of detachment, focusing on delivering excellence without emotional attachment to outcomes. It's your job, it's not YOU. It deserves a piece of you, not all.

KEY TAKEAWAYS

- True power comes from within, not from external factors
- Detach from external validation to reclaim personal power
- Focus on delivering value, not seeking validation

"If you're really open to change, you won't go south this year."

Part III
PURPOSE

[phonetic: **pur**-*puhs*]

noun

1. the reason for which something exists or is done, made, used, etc.
    Synonyms: <u>target</u>, <u>objective</u>, <u>object</u>, <u>rationale</u>, <u>point</u>
2. an intended or desired result; <u>end</u>; <u>aim</u>; <u>goal</u>.
3. <u>determination</u>; resoluteness.
4. the subject in hand; the point at issue.
    | *practical result, effect, or advantage: to act to good purpose*[3]

---

3 "purpose," *Dictionary.com*, 2024, https://www.dictionary.com.

> **PODCAST CLIP: THE SHIFTING NARRATIVE OF BLACK EXPERIENCE WITH JUSTIN SIMIEN**

Justin Simien: Like everyone's like, you know, "We got to make our own Hollywood, our own Black Hollywood." Yeah. But we also, I think first we have to make our own, like, Black art culture.

You're doing it right now, just having this podcast and having these kinds of conversations, but like. Okay, so if you go back to, like, the sixties and the seventies, you can see that the movies are different in the seventies. The reason why, yeah, the studio system collapsed, but also the big reason is a bunch of French dudes got together and they came up with something called *Cahiers du Cinéma*, and they basically decided: We are going to teach people how to watch movies because other critics and reviewers don't know what they're talking about. They're, like, shitting on all the great Hollywood directors like Hitchcock. They don't really know. They're not really talking about it as an art form.

And they just literally got together. These are people like, you know, Godard and like, there was a lot of folks. . . . They basically, like, changed the way movies were seen and then they were able to make the kind of films that did more daring things that really confronted their audiences, that really made you ask, like, what is a movie at all?

Like really brought people into, like, what art cinema was, but it started as a cultural conversation that they were just having about the movies. They basically, like, they opened up the conversation about what cinema is and then they went on to make movies and by the time this is called the French New Wave, eventually it gets to America and it's called, you know, the, the New American Wave and all, but it all starts with a group of people who were like, "Oh, we're just really annoyed with how people are talking about movies. So let's talk about them differently."

16

A REMINDER

So, let's get real for a second. Purpose can feel like this elusive thing that only some people get to have, you know? Like, they're the chosen ones who magically figure it out, and the rest are just over here trying to get by. Or it can feel like this burden that we have to engage with for us to be valid. But I want to challenge that thinking; what if purpose already exists inside and it's simply achieved by you following your heart, whatever that is? It's not necessarily defined by external confirmations. Purpose is just the passion that keeps you going.

For me, my purpose is ignited and informed by my power, which I get through the way I show up for myself and so many others. That may be through performing, teaching my niece how to do her makeup, saying yes to me and no to others, or sharing what I know during a college workshop. This journey I've been on of mastering my mind and reframing my thoughts has been necessary for my survival. The answer is always in what makes you happy. By curating a positive and uplifting environment, you create space for your true self to shine and for your goals and aspirations to unfold with greater ease and reward. My purpose has always been driven by simple and tangible (yet intangible) things like making my family proud, making myself proud, making God proud, and the belief that we're all capable of goodness. And I know that sounds simplistic but having that be my guiding force has led me here.

I have the intense desire to focus on creating more space for goodness while I'm here. And, of course, now I have my son, who I actually popped out of my butt and I love so much. My life is so much more purposeful with him in it!

17

LEO

The moment I got the call to host *Saturday Night Live*, I knew I wanted my baby to make that night his official debut out into the world. I'd been working towards this gig for a really long time. We were about six months out from Leo's arrival. My family and loved ones kept asking me if I was going to release the maternity photos we'd taken with David LaChapelle. That didn't feel right for my baby; a post wouldn't be enough for the bundle I was carrying inside my body. At the same time, speculation was brewing left and right from my Twitter feed to my Instagram stories. People would not stop making comments on the tiniest details under my posts, and I didn't want to give them the power to make me spill the tea. It's my news, damn it!

I remember just being so excited, thinking it was so fun and cool that I was doing all these sketches and rolling, jumping, hopping, and skipping around with my son in my stomach. Like, Son, we did *SNL*. Together. My first time hosting *SNL*, and I got to do it with you. It was the experience of a lifetime. My passion for theater and experience on live studio sitcoms like *True Jackson, VP* really did prepare me for a moment like this.

There are so many reasons why we hold our children so close. As much as I enjoy speculating and kiki-ing with the next person about bits of gossip, there's the reclamation and privacy that I knew I wanted to secure while having my child. It's not like your favorite entertainer is being weird; we're just humans! (So ofc we're weird.) Humans who want to feel ownership of our own good news—which we should 100 percent be entitled to. At least that was how I felt. The problem is that when people watch you so much—and there's nothing wrong with it—they can tell when the slightest thing is different, whether it's how your clothes fit or how you're walking down the street.

And you can get defensive when—sometimes—your good news is really not your good news. As if your good news belongs to the public; it's their good news and they scream it before you can even whisper it. And then it makes you kind of want to hold back even more because you just want to have something that you have control over. There are a lot of people in the industry growing up and starting their own families, and I wish, as a society, we would just go easier on them.

I remember when all the speculation around Halle Bailey's pregnancy first started. I didn't get the idea that she didn't want to tell everybody. I got the idea that she wanted to tell people when she wanted to tell them, because it was her news to tell. You know what I mean? It's not your good news to tell me about me, it's my good news to share when I want to share it with you! Now we have language around what's considered a "hard launch" and a "soft launch," which is actually really cute (and the creativity behind some of these videos and posts are so dope) but the literal definition of "launch" is to promote something. And as a culture, do we need to promote everything we do in private to the public?

Tuning out the opinions of others is a key and crucial skill when it comes to walking a path of purpose. Especially when you are experiencing major personal events in the middle of major career events. Honestly. One of the most annoying things was when people were in my comments saying things like, "Girl, you ain't hiding it from nobody" and "I know baby weight when I see it." It's like, I'm not really trying to hide anything. You think I'm trying to play some game where I'm withholding information, thinking my information is greater than yours? No, I'm just trying to wait for the perfect time to reveal this special occasion out of respect for myself and my son. So when you factor in the public's assumptions and speculations about being pregnant while also actively attending regular doctor check-ins and working through your own anxieties, there's a lot going through your head. And I'm not even going to get into the statistics regarding the maternal mortality rate for Black women. So with all that on my mind, the last thing I intended to do was be tricky. I wanted to be safe. So it's really about tuning out the noise and staying true to yourself and what allows you to be most at peace to complete all the tasks at hand. The rest of the world is screaming about the size of my clothes and how they fit but I'm focusing on the fact that I tripped while walking up some stairs and I hope my baby's okay. I just wanted to make it to the delivery room, and off the delivery table, with my son.

The truth is there are people in your life right now who are distracting you from your purpose by telling you what they think you should do instead of what you want to do. For me, the reality is that my real fans actually don't try to tell me what to do, and I consider them a true blessing and a real fan base. Because most of the people who talk to hear themselves talk aren't looking out for your best interests. Sometimes you can see what people are typing and writing and putting out there and you can think that they're coming from a place that, to them, might feel like they're sharing an apple from the tree in the Garden of Eden. But most of the other people who are aligned with you and think differently aren't saying anything, you know what I mean? Like, there're so many times when I don't agree with or understand what someone I love is saying or doing, but I don't say anything because they didn't ask me. I'm also not in their shoes, so I trust that they know how to handle their own life. No one will agree with everything anyone does; that's the price you pay when you're forging your own path! A lot of the people who do agree with me are also just observers. There are two types of people on the internet: the internet extroverts who enjoy the ability to say whatever is on their mind despite the impact, and the internet observers who seem like they aren't there but they are, just observing and respectfully not commenting because they do respect you and your decisions. They will let you do you.

And, of course, sometimes I'll clap back! But I know when and where to expend my energy. I'm incredibly mindful. The discernment that I had to have as an entertainer was that most of the people who love you and adore you are most likely not saying anything. In fact, many of them might not even be online. (Shocking, there *is* a world where people don't go on social media, who knew?!)

My time on *SNL* felt right for me, and had I taken the time to respond to the noise and what other people wanted from me, which was not on my dime or my time, I wouldn't have had the time of my life on that stage. I reimagined one of my favorite childhood shows with *both* Kenan and Kel. I created an anthem for "Big Boys" with my girl SZA. I was finally able to publicly ask Drake for compensation after wreaking havoc in my life when he dropped "In My Feelings." I delivered an iconic five-minute monologue, adding myself to the ranks of my favorite hosts, including Steve Martin, Eddie Murphy, and Cicely Tyson—the first Black woman to ever host in *SNL*'s history. And along with all this, little did ten-year-old me think I would be whipping out a baby bump mid-speech.

I couldn't have asked for a more perfect reveal.

Children are the light of the world, and my son is the centerpiece of mine. And now I get to see the world through his eyes. I'll do anything for Master Leo.

To be clear, a baby will fucking wreck your life, okay? A baby will make your life so happy even when your relationship, your job, and your mental and emotional energy feel like shit. Obviously, my life was life-ing before my son, but then here he comes, a mini tornado, making me question everything I thought I once knew about my life.

I'm a *MOTHA*. I can stand on business all day, every day, when it comes to my son. In the weeks when we brought him home, I was so scared that something was gonna happen to him that I didn't want to let him out of my sight. But then I had to breathe. I had to tell myself, *Girl, it's okay to love another human being this much.* I said my affirmations. I tried to get with the program.

No one ever talks about postpartum being an indefinite state of mind. People just make it sound like after the standard six to eight weeks, everything should be back to your regularly scheduled programming. But in reality, postpartum is like having mental warfare when you don't even know you're having mental warfare. One second, I could be smiling and laughing with someone, and the next thing that pops in my head is, *Oh my gosh, what if my baby just falls out the window right now and just dies, ha ha, like that would just be so crazy.* And now I'm fighting with myself internally about whether or not it's weird that I just randomly had a thought about my baby falling out the window! And now I also have to be practical with myself, because it's like, yes, girl, that really could happen if you miss a step. In fact, your baby could fall out of your hands right now and die and now, well, let's go back into the house because we actually shouldn't even have taken him out of the crib today and, actually, now I'm scared of the stairs, so let's move to a place with no stairs, because you never know, one day you'll just be coming down the stairs and there goes your baby's delicate neck.

And all this seemed normal to me in the moment, because how could I not think the life I just created could be snatched up from me in an instant? But that's actually just a side effect of the chemical imbalance in my newfound mom brain and the insanity that's created after you have a baby. And that's when I realized I'll forever be postpartum because I am forever changed. My mind is just not working the same anymore—how do I come to terms with that?

There was a lot of paranoia for me at the beginning when I didn't trust nobody with the baby. I remember one time when I had just had my baby and we were staying in Connecticut. My mom kept repeating, "Just lie down, now. You just got back from the hospital. Now lie down, take a nap. We'll watch the baby, we'll watch the baby."

I did try to sleep. And I probably slept for all of thirty minutes, maybe forty, when I woke up sobbing in bed. Darius was trying to comfort me and all I kept saying was, "I want to see Leo."

"Well, he's just in the living room," Darius said.

I couldn't stop crying for the life of me. "But they all want me to rest. Everybody keeps telling me to rest. And I guess I should rest, but I just want to be near him."

Darius said, "It's okay. Just go to the living room. You can be with Leo." And then I went out there.

There were so many intense moments like this. Similarly, there was a moment when friends and family were coming to visit and people kept wanting to hold the baby. It was all harmless stuff, but once I pulled Darius into the back and said that I wanted everyone to leave. I said something like, "I need my mom to stop touching my son!" And I knew it sounded insane, but that was my truth at the time.

Everyone seemed like an op, even Sharon! And I just felt like nobody was getting where I was coming from. They didn't understand. At the same time, I wasn't even telling them anything *to* understand. Sometimes, I think I do *too* good of a job acting like everything is okay and it's hard for others to know I'm not steering my ship.

Inside Out 2 explained anxiety so well, how it can steer the ship of your emotions to the point where *joy* is nowhere in sight. That's how it was for me, I was just acting like everything was okay. Every now and then I would share things with Darius because he was the closest to me as the father of our child. But even then, with him, I was side-eyeing. I felt so guilty for having such selfish feelings about a baby I knew all my family and friends loved, especially his father. I think the terror and the impact you feel when you realize you're the person who cared and created this life in your body, and it genuinely is your responsibility, create unexplainable anxiety. The way I processed the heavy weight when I first became a mom was with so much complete caution, which no one knew I was experiencing. I have this overawareness because I read and I listen, but nothing can teach you better than experience. No article can prepare you for motherhood because it's such a unique experience.

I'm mentally in a better place now than I was before, but I know that some of these intense anxieties are still present, deep inside me. I'm a little bit more leveled out, so I'm able to see things differently and acknowledge my fears. But when your mind and your physical body are experiencing all that chemical imbalance, it's not like an alarm is going off that's signaling, *You're chemically imbalanced!* You don't think about the conversations that you've had with doctors or all the research that's out there about the effects of postpartum. You just know that one day, you don't sound or think like you used to. And that's a bitter pill to swallow.

At the same time—and two things can be true at once—being Leo's mother has empowered me on another level. All it requires is for me to show up the best way I can for him. And I'm willing to do whatever it takes, even vacation, therapy, and whatever else I have to do for myself. All jokes aside, when my baby is good . . . I'm *GREAT*! Have you seen his adorable face?!

18

EMERALD HAYWOOD

The episode is called "Obama Shutdown" and it's the fifth episode of the third season of *Key & Peele*. My guest appearance on the sketch is brief, as I play Malia's Anger Translator after Barack and Michelle (played by Jordan Peele and Mekia Cox) have just finished a conversation using their own anger translators (played by Keegan-Michael Key and Nicole Randall Johnson) to agree to have a night full of intimacy after a long, tedious day of being away from each other. My character comes into frame behind Malia (played by Saba McGee), wearing huge pink hoop earrings and an eyebrow ring and rocking a voluptuous blowout. She is full of attitude, and she delivers her lines with the force to back them up.

"If you don't let me go to this party, I will get a tattoo. On my face."

My first foray into improv comedy can be attributed to this show and this episode, which aired back in 2013. It was fun, and a completely different vibe from what I was used to. I didn't realize it yet at the time, but I was open to bringing a new version of myself to light through this form of entertainment. I was new to sketch comedy, and when the doors opened up for me, I stepped through them. I knew there was something in my spirit that didn't want me to leave sketch comedy, and the timing of this experience meant something greater was in store.

I will never forget the call I got from my managers when they let me know that Jordan Peele wanted to get on the phone with me. They had no idea what it was about. It involved a new film he was doing, but everything was kept under wraps. Jordan is known for being relatively quiet and private about his projects. I was too excited to hear that I was on his radar, and I couldn't help thinking he remembered my persistent spirit when I'd done improv for the first time on his show.

We set a date and got on a call. This was during a time COVID had pretend-ended, if you know what I mean. No one knew what was going on and we were all being told different things, so the timing was weird, but I do remember us getting on our Zoom call. We spent an hour on the call, where he shared themes of the movie with me, but not the overarching plot of the story. Even then, I knew I wanted to be a part of the film because I'd always been an admirer of Jordan's work. From *Key & Peele* to his directorial brilliance in *Get Out* and *Us*. When I first saw *Get Out*, I actually DM'd him saying how we worked together once and I hoped we could again someday. And here he was, telling me about this film, on this video call. I could already feel myself going through this internal transformation within my own sense of being while on that call, so I could only imagine what would happen if I spent more time learning and collaborating with him over the course of several months.

Jordan has a very specific vision for the worlds he creates and the characters who live in them. There is no good or bad, no black-and-white, in that level of consistency. There is only subjectivity. I'm telling you, there are probably several academic articles and dissertations and college essays debating his work, which really does mark a genius creative. I damn sure know the Reddit threads and reviews would be going crazy. To this day I still get questions and comments about the meaning behind the movie we made, and it's so incredible to see how these conversations have evolved even though it came out more than two years ago. And I'm so appreciative for the level of introspection because there would otherwise be nothing for the audience to dive into that would force them to reflect in these thoughtful ways.

I knew working with Jordan would stretch my limits as an improv artist and collaborator and enhance any other skills that needed some fine-tuning in my toolbox. I knew I needed the quiet and the focus to immerse myself into this world, his world. I knew it would be as extreme as holding your breath underwater for two minutes (I don't know about you, but I can't do that easily). I would have to prepare myself to pay attention, and to be led by a leader as confident, as kind, and as modest as Jordan (which he remained the entire time on set).

So I said yes to the opportunity almost immediately.

And this Pisces man really delivered! It was Jordan's ability to be someone you can share an idea with to enhance the vision he set forth while also being someone you trust to make all the decisions. I'm not kidding when I say we'd established this gentle trust with each other, which I've never shared with any creative before. From the earliest days, I could feel that he really wanted me to inform him on Emerald as much as he would inform me on her character. What made her brave? What made her shiver? Who is Emerald in the face of danger, in the face of uncertainty, and on this ranch with her brother, OJ, who she loves, but who she also sometimes clashes with?

It took about four to five months to shoot this film. Our crew worked what's called "French hours," which, believe it or not, don't have anything to do with France. It's a term that basically eliminates a set lunch "break," which meant we would work while eating to keep the momentum going. It was really such an amazing process, which I liked to think everyone enjoyed, because we just kept moving and making progress at all times. There were so many hardworking, dedicated people on set, and someone I had the pleasure of getting to know was Hoyte van Hoytema, who was the director of photography and is known for his brilliant work with director Christopher Nolan (*Interstellar, Oppenheimer, Tenet*—hello?). I'm pretty sure the cast and crew were equally fascinated with each other, which I feel is a testament to the way Jordan treated everyone by trusting and empowering us to do our thing. It made me excited and motivated for the day I step into a director role of this scope to be able to see how he kept us all together while maintaining our respect and adoration. If you saw the film, you know that everyone, both in front of the camera and behind the scenes, gave it their all. And we'd all probably do it again if he called. (*Nope 2*, anyone?)

It was also so special to learn and understand that my point of view did matter. That it does matter. And to this day, I feel like his favorite actor—bye, Daniel!—even though I genuinely believe this is just how he makes everyone feel. I felt heard, I felt affirmed, I felt valued. Working on this movie changed how I saw myself adding value to a character, from the wardrobe, to how my hair was styled, to the language and how I delivered and set the tone for my lines. Simply because Jordan gave me permission. And I felt so empowered by the permission that I saw my best work because of it. That in itself has made me show up in ways I didn't realize I was allowed to.

Working with a director like Jordan allowed me to see I was capable of making choices and taking chances as an actor. It meant I could be a self-starter and not expect everything to be on the page because it simply can't be. Working and rebranding myself in the digital era prepared me in the best ways and informed how I showed up for this film. It taught me how to be self-contained and know how to work as a true collaborator and not just as an employee. It gave me an entrepreneurial spirit, which is what I encourage every single one of us to have—regardless of the industry you work in.

The process of mastering myself began when I was born (obvi!) but by twenty-six, when I learned that my digital impact landed me a role as a *Good Morning America* second-hour host, I realized how powerful I was on my own. I started to see myself as the business I actually am in the industry. ("I'm not a businessman, I'm a business, man!" as Jay-Z said.) And when my awareness was heightened, so was my focus, and my intentionality, as well. When I realized I could be an asset, my perspective shifted.

And for *Nope*, Jordan saw something in me and confirmed to the world that I am indeed an asset to anyone who comes in contact with me. What I did for myself, I could do for and with anyone else. This experience allowed me to reflect on how I'd been doing the yearslong work, practicing my own improv and artistic autonomy through my digital rebirth, which truly prepared me for my role as the multifaceted badass Emerald Haywood. And it was my pleasure.

Timing is real. Everything happens when it's supposed to, so keep carving out the space to do the work.

19

REFRAMING YOUR MIND

The beauty of social media, to me, is when something from the past finds a new life for a different generation. It's always been such an honor being able to be part of someone's childhood, and I don't take it for granted. To this day, I still get people who think my real name is Akeelah, or ask me to spell *prestidigitation*, or wonder if I am really related to Angela (and I might as well be! I love that woman, and I love doing my impression of her so if you haven't heard it yet, Google is your friend). But people growing up in the last ten years may only know me from these viral clips and memes like "Sorry to This Man," or *Hot Ones*, or a film like *Nope*, and I think that's cool, too!

And it really goes back to fans and the people who've cultivated an online community to rally and continuously show artists love.

Y'all remember that limited TV series *Swarm*? I devoured that show in a few days. I loved that it represented stan culture, to its own degree, while also adding elements of compassion, heart, and humanity. (Spoiler alert.) For example, when Chloe Bailey's character, Marissa, becomes the face of Ni'Jah? I felt like what they were ultimately saying was that it wasn't so much that Dre (played by Dominique Fishback) was obsessed with Ni'Jah, but that she'd been through so many ups and downs through the foster care system that the first time she felt like she had family was with Marissa. And the memories of the two of them revolved around attending Ni'Jah concerts and listening to her music. Similar to the concept of the music video for "Stan." Because the truth of stan culture is not that you're obsessed with that person, but you're obsessed with the memories that are attached to that person.

I strongly believe that our memories are the closest things we have to preserving something everlasting in this life, whether it's in digital form or not. People love Michael Jackson's music for this reason. We all have different takes on Michael's career and persona because we've all heard his music for the first time at different points in our lives. My parents had Michael when he was part of the Jackson 5 as a little kid. My era of Michael was the *Dangerous* album with "Black or White" and "Remember the Time." So to know that we will always have artists who become these generational talents because their performances have touched us as they've evolved into different beings also motivates me to continue evolving.

And people pull me back into the past all the time. One day I'll be scrolling through Instagram and the next thing you know, fifty-eleven people will tag me in an old video or something, which will bring back a flood of memories. I remember back in 2020 when the Disney pilot of *Keke & Jamal* resurfaced and started circulating. People couldn't believe the little girl side-eyeing Vanessa Hudgens and being a diva to my play-brother Andre Jamal Kinney. It was so random, but it's really the coolest thing ever, the gift that keeps giving. It's like, damn, you guys are really out here keeping me alive! Like, as I continue to evolve as an entertainer, it's equally memorable to look back on these moments with y'all in real time. I'm sure Jake Gyllenhaal be feeling the same way when he sees all the *Donnie Darko* memorabilia following all over the entire web.

Once, I remember asking Eddie Murphy about stand-up, to which he revealed that it was always a means to an end. That it especially became difficult to do stand-up once people loved him so much. As if being an artist and evolving in his stand-up was solely based on people wanting to bust out of their pants laughing but not even really responding to the material he was performing. Only his stardom more than anything. So it was already cool to see moments in the script that played to the things that people who love Eddie know him for, but it was even cooler to see him work against the grain and ask for different things. Artists should continue testing themselves! You, reading this book, should continue to test yourself! And while I understand the concept of "if it ain't broke, don't fix it," how do you know you're not missing out on discovering something new about yourself? There is also space for this exploration, and as a performer, sometimes I think it's useful just for us.

It's so interesting to have millennial versus Gen Z versus Gen Alpha discussions, because even though the narratives typically pit us against one another with regard to our beliefs and how we grew up in a certain way, I think we can all agree that we're all simply just trying to figure out our place in society.

I was having a conversation with a good friend of mine and we were criticizing a conversation he had with someone who was significantly younger. Not a child but like a young adult. Now, at first we were going in and then something came to us both where we were like, *Wait a minute. Is this a reflection of our age?* Meaning, there is obviously the reality that you share different views with people but then there is also the reality that people can only speak to experiences from their vantage point. When we are younger we have such little information and that doesn't mean our thoughts and feelings are any less real but they aren't as informed. This varies, of course, but I started asking myself if I am right to define that as who they are or if this is just a reflection of their age. Like, can being young be a personality? And is my new perspective about this really a reflection of me growing out of my own youthful persona? I believe that much of who we thought we were growing up wasn't really us—we were just figuring things out. And then when you add in the bold, unapologetic versions of ourselves we presented online through Myspace, AIM, or Tumblr, it's like a jump scare! These digital footprints can resurface at any time, whether we like it or not, and force us to confront the personas we've long left behind. The worst thing is being held to something you said when you were twenty. Like, yes, that's what I said at twenty-one, but shit! I'm thirty-one, and it's called growth! Like, get real!

Listen, I don't want to be that millennial in the corner of a party, sulking like an old hag while people younger than me are bussin' the newest TikTok dance in the middle of the circle. Will I be in the middle of the circle at the party? Probably not. But will I be doing my little two-step around the perimeter and observing? Maybe!

As I've gotten older, I've realized how many things make so much more sense to me now. And in a way, I've actually matured into my personality. A lot of things I did when I was young were not necessarily my personality; they were simply just me being young. Like when I see that my son cries all the time, at first, I think, *I've done everything: he's fed, he's dry, and he's crying again, what's wrong?!* But then I have to remind myself, *Girl, nothing is wrong; he cries because he's a baby. That is what babies do.* In fact, if he didn't cry as much as he did, I would have been even more concerned.

What I'm trying to say is that I've noticed a certain level of resistance to the times changing from my fellow cohort of millennials, especially as a newer, fresher, cooler generation is making their way onto social media platforms and discovering their own voices. And it's funny to see how it's starting to exist within us, this resistance in accepting that not only is society evolving, but so are the workforce, our relationships, our conversations about things like mental health, and so much more. If we're not going to actually change the times, we actually have to change ourselves.

Honestly, I was never afraid of getting older. Maybe it's because I've been a parentified child for so long, I simply couldn't see how it could get any worse, ha! It's like so much of what made me the Keke Palmer you see today is because of what I've done and experienced in my youth and young adolescence. There's actually a part of me that's relieved that certain aspects and memories of my past are way behind me. Like, hell yeah I made some mistakes, learned some lessons, accomplished some major milestones, and *ta-da*! Here I am, still being able to do what I love—which is an absolute blessing by the grace of God.

If you really want to know, my new (unlocked) fear is losing my sense of self as time goes on, as I get older, and I, perhaps, process things differently. It's concerning to think that part of growing older could include losing what makes me feel proud of myself. There's a bit of vanity in there, I'll admit, but it's not even totally about looking like a sexy snack whenever I leave the crib, per se. It's just about feeling good about me, you know? Loving myself and being excited about me in the way that is naturally there when we are "young." I don't want my personality to be totally defined by my age and regeneration. I just wanna love myself at every stage of this journey of life and give myself grace along the ride.

And this is also when I realized I was maturing. There's no despair in my voice when I say, "Wow, I'm getting older." It's really a "Yes, bitch! I'm getting older!" I'm here for it. And not only am I getting older and maturing in my own actions, but I'm also maturing in the way that I've been receiving others. And the way that I'm perceiving others, especially younger people, because they're just young.

Millennials will always have a unique perspective because we grew up in a particular era when social media was coming up. But we also had the experience of being *outside* outside. A lot of the appeal for us has worn off because guess what? We're not the super young ones; now they're studying the kids who grew up in a world where social media and AI already exist commercially. So, the way we're perceiving things, the way we're looking at things, it's not the same as it was when we were in our twenties. And people are not as impressed with our perspective as they were when we were in our twenties because we don't have a youthful outlook anymore. I'm sorry if this is the first time you're hearing this, but it's true! The Gen-Zers are calling the shots and defining culture in a way that should continue to be embraced. Not met with resistance.

And it's also about being honest! For me, one way I stay true to myself is by knowing what's for me and what's not. This involves which social media apps I use. I don't start myself on a new platform and produce content on it unless it feels authentic to me. I think there's danger in spreading yourself across multiple avenues; you just gotta listen to your audience. Which is how I've maintained my own sense of authenticity across all the platforms that I'm a part of. Like, even though I like TikTok, I think I'll forever be an Instagram girlie. I'm telling you there's something I don't trust about TikTok's interface; it doesn't give you space to pull yourself out of the constant stream of videos. And it's also actually really freaking difficult to dance on TikTok, okay?! (Not for me, but like others . . .)

Anyway, all I'm saying is we gotta keep meeting ourselves where we're at. I am trying to actively keep an open mind about the fact that obviously I met a different version of myself at twenty. I'm also meeting a different version of myself now at thirty-one. And I can't wait to meet a different version of myself at forty. And I just wanna be into her—whoever she is.

So my plan is to keep staying engaged and to not lose the personal investment I'm making in myself as I continue to come into

Keke 2.0, 3.0, and on. Pivots and reinventions don't have to come from a place of fear. Keeping up with the times and the culture through conversations, whether digitally or in person, is key. Choosing to do something different from time to time is important and should be exciting! Who's with me?

20

A STUDENT OF LIFE

Being honest with yourself and others is hard. As someone who's built a platform on being as authentic as possible, I don't lie to myself, and I don't lie to other people. Like, I just don't do it. Now, if your hair looks terrible, I may grapple with that one, but that's not a real lieeeee. My Virgo self is naturally a curious person, so my favorite questions when I'm inquiring more about something someone has said are typically things like, "Oh, but what's that mean?" Or, "You know, I don't understand that." Or even, "Can you describe that?" And I found out very early that my candor is what felt very endearing to other people.

I've built a reputation of not being afraid to say what I don't know. I don't know what I don't know! And that's on Communication 101, period. This really applies to any aspect of my life—whether that's with TV executives or my own siblings. It's not part of my performance; it's not something I'm trying to do to be charming. I just have no other choice but to say, "Hey, you know what? I don't know that." My goal in life has been to remain genuine and curious. I hold these traits very close to me because I want people to know that I want to keep learning.

(Why do you think I started a podcast? Baby, this is Keke Palmer!)

And as much as I still want to keep learning, I do know there are times when I could still be a bit self-sacrificial, faltering to old habits. It happens! The other day I had to be honest about my apprehensions on a particular project because I was being dishonest with myself about what I really thought about my commitment. I allowed other people's thoughts, needs, and feelings about the project to influence my decision, even though I'd made a promise to prioritize only things that I truly wanted to spend time on and invest my craft in. Because of the constant boundaries I'd been setting to prioritize myself and my kid's well-being—along with getting older, having a baby, going through a public separation, etc.—it's easier for me to cut through the bullshit and say, "Hey, this doesn't feel right to me."

Investing in your personal growth is all about consistency. Get into it, loves.

21

I FORGIVE YOU. AND I FORGIVE MYSELF.

It's true: people will disappoint you. And it's also true: you will disappoint people. And a third thing, because you're not off the hook from yourself: you will disappoint you.

All these things are okay. And allowing space for all these feelings to exist at once only further shows how nuanced we are as human beings.

There was a point in my life when my family encouraged me to reject my fame and power, because they were afraid it was going to usurp them. It sucked that the people who knew me best credited my sense of pride to my fame, when, in truth, my self-pride has always come from within, since birth. I'll always be Keke Palmer. That's always who I've been, even before I was famous. And from that experience, I knew I didn't need to be around people like that; I didn't want to be around people who are afraid of my light.

But I do acknowledge my beautiful life was also complicated. Due to traveling and scheduling, both my parents had to stop working to support my career and be present for my three siblings, leaving me unassumingly with the financial responsibility around age twelve. Which I took great pride in, because I knew what it would do for generations to come, and it was a huge blessing that I could even help out. However, it caused me a lot of pain because I essentially had to abandon my childhood feelings and desires and become this parentalized child with a lot of weight on my shoulders, which is something I've talked about and I'm sure some of you can probably relate to in your own way. This is something that I've had to continuously work through because while I am grateful, I often feel like I missed the "IT" factor of life.

Life can be such a tragic comedy because we forget to laugh through it, and then it's gone. Now that I am an actual parent, this responsibility I've always carried is more valid than ever, and it's given me the chance to feel what it's like to be a kid again. I get a chance to explore a lot of the things I missed out on with my son. His freedom is, like, the most priceless gift to me. He is already teaching me so much; it's like he awakened the little me inside who I thought was long gone, the irony.

And to this day, my siblings and I are very close. I love watching them and my nieces and nephews form bonds with my Leo Beo. I will always be grateful that we are always there for one another and that our parents raised us to know how to live without them. They worked really hard to instill that tight bond between us and it gives me comfort that I'll never be alone on this earth. And I know the importance of not just family but of being there as an active family member. We don't even have to say anything to each other. My family's superpower is that we're intuitive as hell, and we know when we need to be around and can tell when someone is struggling. We ask no questions, we just show up. We are like a mafia.

Forgiving is hard, but it's something I've learned that has been helpful for me, because turning thirty meant evaluating and putting so many things in perspective. I've fallen out of relationships and friendships before, but there was a point in my life when I felt like I had to release a friend who I worked with. The lines were blurred as we were building these stepping stones to success. But there came a time where I just couldn't trust him.

I think back on our friendship, and I hate how I left things. I've always had a problem believing that I can trust or depend on people, and I think a lot of this apprehension created these unrealistic standards. So when someone doesn't reach these standards, especially when a mistake is made, it proves that. The sad part is that, at the end of the day, it's really not on the other person as much as it's about how I felt about myself. Work was one thing, but our friendship was more than that. In hindsight, I knew he was going through a tough time personally and, as a friend, I could've shown more compassion. But I just didn't know how to communicate that with him, so I lashed out when I treated everything as if it was business only. I know it must've been hurtful on the receiving end. The truth is I do love him and appreciate him for being the graceful and beautiful human being who was in the trenches with me. We didn't need to keep working together for me to be a good friend and supporter.

So if you ever get a chance to read this, I'm sorry for not handling you with greater care because despite it all, you were doing your best and giving your all and I know you were doing it because you cared for me. To have discarded the relationship entirely was not okay. I think about all the fun we had, all the good times. They will always mean so much to me. I hope that you are doing well, and from the looks of it, you're killing it. I'm rooting for you from afar, Mr. You Know Who You Are.

If you wanna reach new heights, honey, you gotta dig deep—spiritually and emotionally. Are there people in your life you feel like you need to release your emotions to? Even if you don't extend the olive branch directly, maybe you do this in your Notes app or in your own journal. Write a letter. Detail the experience from your end. Consider what they were going through, too. Release those thoughts you're holding in your body.

22

BIG BOSS

Big Boss was both the title of my last album and my directorial debut. Honey, I spent $300,000 of my own money to produce it and thankfully sold it to Amazon for a period of time, under an undisclosed amount, so I was able to pay myself back and earn a little extra. This was the biggest investment I'd ever made in myself, on myself, for my brand and my legacy. I was terrified moving around those big numbers to get to where I needed to be. But people like the Wayans brothers and Tyler Perry gave me permission to invest in myself in this way and showed me that this was all possible. Creating this project independently and then selling this work was a great, strategic way to make even on an investment and maintain creative control. Similar to the conversation on owning your own masters in the music industry, holding on to your IP is really a whole different book in itself.

This movie represents so much of my own personal story and testimony in finding myself and learning to value my creativity over anyone else's, which was easy in every medium but music. I had an incredibly traumatic experience creatively with music so early on that it stifled my sense of artistry. But when I look back on those years, I always had a clear sense of who I was. Even the cover of my first album, *So Uncool*, was four different photos of me in different vibes, as if I was already displaying different personalities, which was so kitschy and so me. The concept of being "cool" is defined by so many specific factors that I honestly never wanted to participate in. And the quirkiness in playing with character and identity was so rich for me—even at the age of thirteen.

Big Boss is about me owning and sharing the process of getting there through themes of horror, while touching on self-reflection and narrative storytelling. And narrative storytelling is the literary tool I find the most impactful to get this message across. Maybe this is because of my upbringing through Biblical stories, but whether it's done through film or music, the use of character and creating a narrative arc from the beginning to the end have always been fulfilling feats for me. *Big Boss* was the first time I was able to combine my skills in this way while collaborating with such an extraordinary team, and all this left me feeling a bit emotional. And even though I'd been shunned and deterred from participating in the music industry in other ways before, this movie was me coming back to myself and validating what I always knew: I will always be the Big Boss in my life.

23

IT'S ALL ABOUT PATIENCE

These days, I have to remember how to surrender and have patience. I am someone who processes things very quickly. I am a quick processor in conversation because of my ADD. But I think problems have been created a lot of the times in my life because I'm expecting everyone to process things the same way I do. And then when they don't it's like there's this judgment on who they are as people, when they're just different. Like, either they'll get there or they were never meant to, but whichever it is, it's okay, they're on their own time. I've fallen into this with my own family. I've fallen into this with my chosen family. I've learned to meet people where they're at and not hold them to my own random standard because we're humans and we're not a monolith. Like, if I get something that somebody else doesn't get, instead of being frustrated they don't see it my way, I've learned to be more open to their vantage point. Because sometimes in my quick processing, maybe there's something I've missed. I'm a big-picture person, *see the forest for the trees*—type vibe, but what if it's the trees that need inspection? Perspective is on the individual; I don't want my impatience to make anyone feel bad or judge their intelligence or judge who they are off that. You can actually just meet them where they're at. I don't know that I realized it was patience needing to be used there, and not on the other person but me with myself and how I make space for our differences. Why should I be more harmful?

That doesn't actually change anything. If you're always that person who can see the forest for the trees easier than others, you don't then use that against anyone, or make people feel bad for that, or judge their intelligence or judge who they are off that. You can actually just meet them where they're at. So showing patience has always been big for me, and I encourage you to evaluate your own relationship to patience.

I haven't started teaching this to my son because he don't really know, but I've been doing small things. "Hold on, wait a minute," I'll say. Sometimes he can be a bit of a boss baby. Obviously, he gets it from his mama. But also he's an only child and the firstborn. So sometimes I have to remind him that everybody can't jump for him all the time. Sometimes he has to wait! But as of right now, that boy gets everything he wants most of the time because he's just the tutest twiddle tingggg.

When he gets older and starts talking more, I'm definitely gonna be teaching him not only patience, but what it means to be kind and polite. It excites me to raise him this way because he is going to be someone who has privilege and I want him to know early on how much good he can do with that.

And even as I continue to perform, this time it's not through the lens of what others want me to be, but who I'm deciding to be. At the end of the day, aren't we all putting on a performance? The gag is, who's pulling your strings?

Tuning out the opinions of others is a key and crucial skill when it comes to walking a path of purpose. Especially when you are experiencing major personal events in the middle of major career events.

No one is going to tell you *how* to empower yourself, but I want to tell people how to empower themselves with the truth. Because if you don't know how the system works, you can't make it work for you.

The truth is everybody doesn't have to like what you do for you to be successful with it. It really doesn't matter who hates it; what really matters more is who likes it. There is an audience for everything, so please keep doing your thing.

If the door's not opening, I'm gonna bulldoze through it. By any means necessary, you know what I mean? I can't give more energy into why it's the first door that's being bulldozed through. I just know I'm gonna take those doors down and I'm also gonna take whoever the fuck wanna come with me. And that's how I step into my power.

There's this misconception about darkness always being the worst and ugliest moments of your life. And I'm here to tell you something you probably don't want to hear: the best things are brewing during your darkest hours. How you make it through the darkness will inform your purpose, and I encourage you to embrace it.

I started becoming an artist in a way that felt fun and natural to me. It was also liberating because I was calling the shots, and it was freeing that nobody could tell me they did or didn't like it.

Society loves to tell us what's of value, but the true fear is not in taking the bait and believing you're worthless; it's actually in believing that you are worthy, important, and capable. Because once you know this, you have to *be* that in action.

The other day, I was starting to teach him what it means to give back. My baby has so many toys and so many clothes. He's a growing boy—he don't need all that! I think it's important for me to teach him from an early age how to balance out all the ways he's blessed. He has grandparents and parents who love him. He has aunts, uncles, cousins, and extended family who will actually fight for him. There's so much love surrounding him that it makes me emotional, and I just never want him to take that for granted.

24

THE FIRST MONDAY IN MAY

André Leon Talley hailed the Met Gala as "the Super Bowl of fashion events," and receiving an invitation meant sitting at the intersection of art, business, entertainment, and—of course—fashion with the most historic players of the industry. I didn't really understand the importance of the Met Gala or what it stood for before I attended. For an outsider, it had a little air of elitism. Kinda pretentious and uncomfortable. Regardless of the night's theme, it can seem very extra. What was a little girl from Robbins like me doing on the red carpet?

Fundraising and charity work aside, the gala is such an artistic showcase of the most creative and innovative minds in fashion and the people who love that world. It's the official opening of the annual fashion exhibit at the museum. It's also about advertisements for brands like Michael Kors, Marc Jacobs, Versace, LVMH, and so many more. Investors, designers, celebrities, politicians, entrepreneurs, the media, the paparazzi—everyone and their mama is tuned into the biggest night of fashion.

It wasn't a surprise that the first time I attended the gala in 2021, I was invited to be the host on the Met's live-streamed red carpet. My look, designed by Sergio Hudson, paid homage to *the* Diana Ross since the dress code was "In America: A Lexicon of Fashion." I loved actively having something to do with all the nerves in my body. And the fact that I was given the creative liberty to bring my personality to every interview I conducted was kismet. If you look at those clips on *Vogue*'s YouTube, you can see the excitement on my face whether I was laughing it up with my girl Saweetie or driving down memory lane with Timothée Chalamet.

The second time I went to the gala was two years later, again dressed by Sergio Hudson. I loved every second of being his muse—from the makeup to the hair to the fabulous dress—and I'm forever honored that we got to continue our narrative on the biggest night of fashion. From the very beginning, Sergio was someone who pushed me to not feel like such an outsider in the fashion world. At the time, I'd never fully felt embraced by fashion because I didn't fit in in terms of what they wanted me to look like. I expected fashion to work in favor of those who were either extraordinarily thin or incredibly desirable, and I didn't feel like I fell into either of those categories.

The confidence Sergio instilled in me when he approached me about being his muse for the second year really changed my life. He compared me to the likes of Robin Givens and Lola Falana. "You are fashion to me," he said, "and you are the woman that I make clothes for, the everyday beautiful businesswoman. You're the woman I want to represent me and my brand."

Sergio may not have known this at the time he was saying these things to me, but his words really became a motivational, guiding light. I just felt really seen, and it was so important for me to be seen in this way, in this time of my life. I'd just given birth and was forty pounds heavier than I'd ever been. Then insert this brilliantly creative man saying I'm the girl, and I'm the one, and you know, he has this assurance in me that made me want to walk taller. I was not what fashion told me I had to be, so I just kind of relinquished everything to him, and was like, "Well, teach me. You tell me what it is." He didn't hesitate to hold my hand and encourage me the whole way through. And it was important that he didn't want or try to change who I was; instead, he said, "No, this is what fashion can be." And we collaborated from there.

Channeling Diana with Sergio was the first step, the beginning of what I didn't know was coming. In my second year at the Met Gala I had all these newfound postpartum curves and the confidence to really acknowledge that I, Lauren Keyana Palmer, could offer something to the fashion world. I could expand my brand in a space that felt intimidating because I'd always thought it was generally not for people like me. And as soon as we stepped onto the carpet, people were *living*. The theme was "Karl Lagerfeld: A Line of Beauty," so our vision blossomed into a dress that was an ode to Josephine Baker, old Hollywood, and Karl's innovative work with Chanel in the '90s. Sergio pushed me to 1) have fun (which we did) and 2) walk around and really talk to people.

My partnership with Sergio marked a new era for me to continue to build camaraderie and lean into the art of collaboration through fashion. It was like an evolution of me that came out of my personal growth and becoming a mother to my wonderful baby boy. This was a pattern I continued to notice as I evolved deeper into motherhood. I'd shed my anxieties and fear of not having a place in certain fields. My motto really became *Look, I ain't got no time for the bullshit. This is what it is.* And it was.

The attitude and energy I felt towards fashion was something I'd never even thought was possible. *Fun* doesn't even feel like a word that encompasses all the joy radiating from my body. From that moment on, Sergio became my creative director, my go-to person for anything fashion related. He does all my tours with me, my photo shoots, like, you know, we do every creative thing together because he is somebody who helped me understand that world. *Essence* dubbed us the "dynamic duo . . . keeping it clutch and leaving no crumbs on the table" in our 2023 cover shoot for their iconic fashion issue and I couldn't agree more.

The call that Marc Jacobs wanted me to be his muse for the 2024 Met Gala gagged me just a tinge, whew! You mean Jacobs by Marc Jacobs for Marc by Marc Jacobs in collaboration with Marc Jacobs for Marc by Marc Jacobs wants Keke Palmer to be one of the girls to represent his brand for the night? Alongside Karol G, Dua Lipa, *and* Venus Williams?

When you go to the Met Gala, the goal is to continue working with different fashion designers and for them to live through you. It's really a collaboration of two worlds. It was a bittersweet moment to not step onto the carpet again in one of Sergio's designs, especially because it's really all quite financial. Going to the Met Gala can be great for exposure but it's not a cheap ad! They need money to maintain the museum! The truth is fashion costs those who like to create it, and Sergio, as a truly independent brand not backed by one of the major companies, has to afford it all on his own. And for this Met Gala, it was in the best interest of his brand not to invest in being present that year. The opportunity for me to break through new heights in fashion almost felt like I was leaving him behind, but he pushed me forward.

"I told you that you could be that girl," he said. "I wanted these things for you, for everyone to see and know that you are that. I'm gonna be there every step of the way. You know I'm always gonna encourage you and you're gonna go kill this."

It was such a blessing that Sergio wanted this moment for me.

And he was there! Before I left, he made sure my nails and hair were on point. He was working with the Marc Jacobs team. He was just so supportive in making sure I was good and he really didn't leave my side. I'm his little niece-slash-daughter-slash-muse. I'm so grateful that he showed up for me. This moment for me ultimately meant it was a win for both of us. All year long we'd trusted each other's visions and taken fashion risks and for Marc Jacobs, who is iconic, to welcome me into the biggest night of fashion (again), and my dearest Sergio, is something I'll forever hold close to my heart.

The theme was "Sleeping Beauties: Reawakening Fashion," which meant the dress code was "The Garden of Time." Everything was centered around fashion of the past. But that could be taken so many ways, and that's the point, ha! The absolute best team worked their wonders beginning at eleven a.m. I pulled up in the highest, sleekest ponytail. Had gemstones all up in my eyes, on my edges, on my neck. My dress, made up of what seemed to be tattered fabric, was indicative of all the beautiful, one-of-a-kind pieces held in the museum. It was so cool that these pieces were unraveling and falling apart, yet their beauty still stood the test of time. What an evolution for myself, but even more for this special collaboration that wouldn't have happened without Sergio's belief in me years earlier.

It was in that moment, as well as when I went to the Webby Awards a few days after and won the Webby Special Achievement Award, that I'd turned to my best friend and said, "I think my impostor syndrome is gone." Which was such a huge deal after everything I'd gone through up until that point. It was the feeling that I belonged in every room I was invited to. I deserve to be everywhere I am, and truly owning it. No guilt or humiliation posed as humility.

The rest of the night was so fascinating. Randomly, one of the waiters decided to take me to the back room. I guess he assumed I was one of the hosts because the back room was their VIP area. I delighted myself with a few hors d'oeuvres and ran into Scott Barnes. We started yapping and in walked Jennifer (Lopez) and her producing partner, a friend of mine I'd met on the set of *Hustlers*, Elaine Goldsmith-Thomas. The thing I love 'bout Jennifer is she DGAF. Straight up, she wanted a beat so she took a beat, OKAY! And the Met can be strict on what they want you to do, when they want you to do it, and with stern grace she took her time. Bad Bunny was there looking like Zorro, quiet but cool. I felt like we were kicking it back there forever! But I honestly enjoyed it; it was a lot of energy in there and I liked seeing Jennifer respond the way she did because it's a reminder to control the pace for yourself. Allow yourself a beat, especially when you're going in front of folks. Once all collected, we walked out together. After I got into the main party, I was sitting at my table, learning more about Marc Jacobs and really getting more insight about how the night is really for the fashion kids, the designers, the sponsors. Everyone in an adjacent industry is here to pour into this moment, their moment. My third go at the Met Gala and I was absorbing what it meant to be an extension to the brands you walk the carpet with.

I had so many genuine moments I didn't expect to have. I remember Nicki Minaj pulling me to the side, sharing this profound and beautiful message with me from her heart that I'll never forget. So I was at my table and I saw Marc and his hubby, Charly, talking to Nicki. I decided to walk over because, through friends, Nicki had hooked up my pregnancy photos. I wanted to thank her again in person but as I approached she was like, "You! Girlie, I need to talk to you, just wait right here," and I was like, "Okay." So Charly was all, "I didn't know you and Nicki were friends." I was in my head like, *Shit, me neither* (LMAO), not like this at least. Like, what she got to say to me? So they finished up their quick conversation while I was standing there positively anxious. Then she sat me down and proceeded to say, "Don't ever let anybody online, on the street, in this world that doesn't understand who we are outside of what it is we do, don't let them tell you what's right for you. And this may not apply to your life. This may have nothing to do with who you are right now. But I just felt like, it was something for me to tell you that nobody knows what it's like for us when all the lights are over. And whatever makes you feel good, never forget to hold that and never let go."

I sat with Nicki's words for a long time because damn! How did she know what I needed to hear? The truth of the matter is that nobody else really can. Not even my mom, not my sister, not my brother—nobody in my life who I trust intrinsically knows what it's like to live a life anything like Keke Palmer's. But you know who might? Nicki Minaj.

Because even though she's not me and I'm not her, someone like Nicki knows what it's like for the world to always weigh in, to always be under a microscope, for people to always have something to say about you, who you are, what you are, what you do, and how your life should be, and what you got to do, and all this madness. To know that being someone who has this weight of being someone people look at doesn't mean that we don't get to make decisions in our personal lives that are for us and us only. And throughout the night I had so many revelatory conversations like this, whether they came from Jennifer Lopez or Venus. And if it wasn't conversations, it was just pure love from all these people I deeply admire. I remember seeing my play auntie Queen Latifah, who was one of the first people who I met very early on in my career and who showed me what it meant to be a queen, to be an example of power and privilege, in the right way. I've been really blessed to have a lot of those experiences with people I was around, people who knew how to handle their success and who set the tone for how I want to be to the young people coming up after me. Not like they told me how to be, but they showed me it's okay for them to be them in the same way that it's okay for me to be me. I'll still shine, maybe even more.

Looking back on my first Met Gala, my relationship to the event was more about keeping myself busy, talking to as many people as I could on the carpet, because when I'm anxious it's better to just do rather than be. Honestly, I was just getting through the night. Everyone's trying to do their part without collapsing on the red carpet and the whole thing can be extremely taxing and overwhelming. I mean, it was still enjoyable for me because my personality and my flamboyance are defense mechanisms. Like a character I create who helps me cope with whatever intensity. Where somebody might get quiet and become guarded, I become the opposite. I get loud and excited. It's what allowed me to balance out the elephant in the room, which was my self-doubt in the periphery of my vision. It's like I knew why I was there, but still found myself questioning why I was there.

This time around, yes, I still wanted to get through the night without busting my ass, but I felt myself being more present in ways I hadn't been. I wanted to connect and learn more about people on a different level. Turning thirty, being a mother of a one-year-old, feeling affirmed by myself and looking hella good while doing it—I felt like I had more room to breathe and have fun.

And there were so many real, down-to-earth people around, even though it's an incredibly star-studded event. At the end of the day, I'm such a deep admirer of the work Anna Wintour has done curating this kind of experience. From the seating arrangement to the no phones and no guests rules, she really wants to force you to have those intimate kinds of connections where you can be yourself. For your most authentic, expressive self to shine.

25

I'M BLESSED TO DO THIS

I've always felt like it was my duty to use my platform wisely, but I never felt the desire to speak on things I don't know enough about.

I group activism in a few different categories. There is social media activism, actual activism, and performative activism. First, there's social media activism, which, in my opinion, is rooted in word of mouth. It's an acknowledgment. It's spreading the word and making people aware of the topic at hand, which is an important aspect of activism, because people can't care about what they don't know about. Then there's actual activism, which I attribute to people who are on the front lines of change, on the ground, organizing with mutual aid collectives, working with legislators, creating platforms to have an open form of conversation and following it up with action, and so much more. Then there is performative activism. To me, this is what we see the most these days. Where people hide behind the idea of caring about a person, place, or thing just to leverage their platform or make it seem like they care about a topic that they don't know enough about. This performative aspect can also feel self-righteous if you actually are being an on-the-ground activist, and it's really discouraging to witness.

I bet if you think about it right now, you can remember a certain time when you witnessed a performative act. For me, the performance that I remember the clearest was when everyone posted black boxes with their #BlackoutTuesday during 2020. In my head, while looking at all these damn black boxes, I was wondering, *Do Black lives really matter now? Is this all it took? Some black boxes and a hashtag?* It was so confusing. I think I even had me a little black box post, wondering why the pressure to post was so heavy and yet that wasn't an actual solution. (Y'all, we gotta find out whose idea it was to flood everyone's feed with a black tile. For real.)

See, even though I want to use my platform that way, I don't feel like everybody needs to or should. We're in this day and age when everyone wants to make others feel like they have to save the world and they can't. Even if you were Bill Gates, you couldn't save the world because half the problems revolve around money and sustainable resources and the other half is—you guessed it—us. Someone might say, well, the lack of knowledge creates the ignorance that leads to us not knowing what's best for us, but even then, no one always does what's best for them! I don't care if they're geniuses. Humans are always up against ego and flesh. We are never going to be on the same page.

So as much as I love and believe in activism, I feel like the greatest form of it is being authentic and caring about what you care about and focusing on the things that ring most true to you. That's what I do! I can't do everything, and even the things I do, I know them to be enough. They're honest and true, and for me that's all that matters.

Earlier I mentioned that I ask many questions and I've been this way since I was a child, chile. I'm a student of life and will always be a student of life. I never want to be someone who thinks they're too good to not ever learn something new because I'm always learning something new, especially about communities I'm not affiliated with. My parents are the kind of people who have always taught me to stand for something bigger than myself. It began with going into communities and schools and doing speaking engagements at colleges at the age of twelve, just so that I was empowering those around me in the different spaces I went into. And when you combine how my learnings come from experiences and conversations I have with others, you get something like *Baby, This Is Keke Palmer*.

People have always loved to hear me talk, and I know that sounds insane and conceited, but it's true! I think it speaks to my work as a child and the maturity I had to acquire to really immerse myself in these gigs. I should call it the *True Jackson, VP* Effect because, really, that's what it is. I just knew early on that I had a way with language and the people around me knew it, too.

The other day, my sister spoke to me about Jacques Lacan, who was a French psychoanalyst, psychiatrist, and doctor in the 1900s. We spoke about his theories on language, which really resonated with me simply because language is beyond words. What *love* means to me isn't necessarily the same as what *love* means to you.

So when I think about language, I also think about attitude and inflection because these are all necessary tools for communication. Being a millennial and being around adults all the time in the corporate and entertainment industry schooled me with certain high-level jargon that I needed to know in order to understand what was going on around me. Not literally; I wasn't walking around with a dictionary in my pocket, but I really had an intuitive sense about what was going on. I had to balance maintaining the essence of a child while communicating my needs to an adult effectively in a way that they could understand. Especially since kids don't like when they can't see themselves in you and no adult likes a kid who can't be a kid. It's like code-switching.

Very early on, while I was doing this child-slash-adult dance, I was also very much doing the Black-girl-in-a-white-world dance at the same time. Maintaining the essence of my culture so that those of my culture could recognize me, while also representing my culture and creating spaces for us elsewhere would require a different language and sensibility that I was actually fine with understanding. Because at the end of the day, I knew it wasn't me who was changing, only the perception of who I was.

See? No one can really know you like you do. And I like to think that this all ties in to how we're all performing a version for ourselves in the world. However, the reason for your performance should solely rely on what your goals are, regardless of how broad or specific, because this drives intentionality and keeps you in control. So being clear on you is the best thing you can do, because then, no matter what you do or where you go, you will always know how to manage how you are perceived and how to manipulate your avatar-self in ways that help you navigate perception.

Our external, world-facing persona can never truly be the entirety of who we are because that's crazy to expose and also not possible! And that's okay, but when you depersonalize and are objective in that way, it becomes easier to manage being perceived. It's then more about the fact of how you can better equip yourself and your avatar to communicate effectively not for people's approval but for your own goals.

I've digressed to give you all these gems, but to even take it back to *Akeelah and the Bee*, the biggest and most profound takeaway is this little Black girl finding language as a way to free herself and her ability to express how she feels. When Dr. Larabee thinks he has her figured out, not only does Akeelah use words to express herself, but she uses words and embraces the definitions of what they mean in her delivery. Words are powerful in this way, and when you add in performance while articulating your needs or intention, this births purpose.

From all the roles I've played up to now, I was learning the power of performance and knowledge and how they could be used to service not only myself but others as well. Like I said, being curious and asking questions and not being afraid to learn is probably my greatest skill. And I wanted to share this knowledge in a more accessible way than, say, daytime TV, which not many people my age or younger are actually tuned in to. (I still live for Daytime Keke though, don't get it twisted!) And between the format—whether that's through audio or video—and the reach, I knew my audience would continue to learn something from my guests and me.

And my podcast definitely gives Regina George's mom's "I'm a cool mom" energy, because we do incorporate something incredibly different. With a podcast, there is no standard or set format; you're kind of finding it and styling it around your vibe. Which is why you'll see a different setup from the first season to this most recent one, and different camera lenses, and possibly live shows, which are always fun. Another thing that's also fun? The fact that my mother has actually become her own character to the world in the Keke Universe. People often comment on my relationship with Sharon because it's like we are sisters. And she makes an incredible effort to understand my language and I hers. (When I first heard my mother say "Period, pooh," I was shook!)

It's always been important to me to bridge that gap because I think I'm pretty old-school with the "respect your elders" gag. I truly do think nothing is new, and even if the resources are, the game hasn't changed. To me it's important to lean on our elders and learn from them while also teaching them new ways to update their old ideas. It's not that they didn't try to make it happen back then; we just have different and more accessible resources now. I've been able to use this really special platform to show that grace and respect to my mother, and hopefully it's encouraging all y'all to have more courageous intergenerational conversations across the board. Life is short! Go ahead and ask your grandpa how he was getting down in his twenties, or your aunt if she likes BDSM, or your father if he ever stole a single thing in his life!

And I apply my love for these conversations with my own mom to all the guests who I've invited to participate on the show. I'm always learning something new from each and every one of them. And I'm very intentional with the fact that I don't just talk to celebrities, but people who are experts of the world and are popular in their field, whether that's having a conversation with Justin Simien, creator of *Dear White People*, on the growing and nuanced conversations in the

Black community and how that's represented through art, or catching up with Jesse McCartney and discussing what it means to find purpose in our passion at a young age, and how it impacts the state of being and existence.

My battles with impostor syndrome disappeared by the time I accepted the Webby Special Achievement Award. It's always awesome to enter a space and know you're not just taking up the space that exists but carving a lane for yourself. So much goodness and abundance had been filtering into my life in different ways. And it's just the beginning, but I'm still learning, and I'm really excited to grow and learn alongside my audience. These things are never easy to put on; the balance of what corporate wants and what you want to do will always be difficult, but I'm so grateful to those who continue to show up every week to listen, because it is an investment and I know y'all want your return!

Truly, I'm blessed to do this.

26
KEYS TO THE CULTURE

Sharing the keys to the culture is my greatest gift and my greatest dream. It all started with a nine-year-old girl who chose to believe in herself. So this is for you and for us, from me.

I really didn't know what to do until I started making my own content, getting personal with my audience and using my traditional experience to make my content unique, digitally. That was the evolution of the Keke Palmer brand, and, in that, I learned the power of advertisers when it came to financial freedom and the power of digital analytics as it pertained to traditional entertainment. When it comes to ads, our community has the hardest time catching the eyes of major brands, and I wanted to create a launching pad to change that. When it comes to analytics, many digital artists don't have the connections or knowledge to make use of those insights in a corporate environment. I want to be a conduit to help change that.

KeyTV is a network in the literal and figurative sense. It is first a community for us to relate, create, and thrive. But it's also a space that leverages my experience, connections, and brand to shine a light on all the brilliant creatives we have always had. It, to me, is a door that leads to power and ownership that has always been there; we just needed a key to unlock those doors. And by "we," I do mean the millennial generation of Black people and people of color. That doesn't mean if you aren't a person of color that you are not welcome in this space. It's actually the opposite: you are welcomed and encouraged to support this space that is centering the voices of marginalized people. Imagine a modern-day platform that embodies the spirit of BET's founders, Sheila and Robert L. Johnson, that leverages the digital space. While the content is there, content isn't the sole focus, it's the icing on the cake—a way to amplify and celebrate community leaders who are driving tangible growth and progress. (That feels like a dash of PBS, too, ha!) Regardless of your background or location, KeyTV invites you to be an active participant in shaping the future of our culture. I'm not apprehensive about being specific in what the brand of the network is; I feel empowered to express it because I think it's something people want to see. I think people, especially millennials, want to be a part of pushing things forward in a way that is truly inclusive. We are in an era where companies are now championing ideas like #BuyBlack. That's progress to me.

KeyTV is a hybrid organization that operates at the intersection of a platform (manifesting an app!), a network, and a foundation. It serves as a platform by showcasing and amplifying innovative content, a network by connecting creators and resources, and a foundation by providing support, funding, and incubation for projects and initiatives that advance digital freedom and democratize filmmaking. It means having a system of leadership that implies that the creators are also the clients. It means supporting without exploiting, especially knowing that this is a system that continues to feed itself as long as we continue to grow it. It never needs to take from itself because the creation and perspectives are abundant and the space breeds that abundance. I tapped into the people around me who were the best at what they did.

Working on a business with friends can be tricky. I've been there, and the entanglements can be dangerous. I've lost business relationships and, more importantly, friendships in a way that has never really sat well with me. As a certified workhorse, I think it's important to find delineating factors that help me unplug. So while I don't often have friends who I work with, when it came to navigating this territory with my peers in KeyTV, I tried to unplug with them in spaces that feel totally outside of what we do. And I challenge myself not to talk about work at all, especially when we're off. I also encourage the team to take time to recharge, refuel, and spend their time for and to themselves. This is a job that doesn't have set hours; it can be the kind of job where you can work seventy-two hours straight if you aren't careful. So, for me, it's important to do things and go places that don't trigger me to perform. And I don't necessarily mean perform as an entertainer; I mean that it's almost too easy to hang around this job that I love. But to gain perspective, I have to actively work to step outside the bubble and do something completely different.

The thing I love the most about all the people I work with

at KeyTV is that they're a team of entrepreneurs and self-starters, which is essentially what KeyTV is all about. We call our partners "KeyMakers" because we have the keys! I'm thrilled about this next chapter, as I've seen firsthand the impact of thoughtful sponsorship through my work with big companies. I've often been the face of their philanthropic efforts, representing the beneficiaries of their investments. Now I'm excited to become the storyteller; it's a woven narrative of growth, empowerment, and the importance of paying it forward. And with God's guidance, it will be done.

Nora and I met at AwesomenessTV, which, in many ways, served as the inspiration for KeyTV. It was a digital network that also worked as an agency. It helped to connect talent with brands and worked with brands to fund digital work. She worked as my product manager while we were both there and helped me produce my show *That's the Gag* and a few others. Personally, she creates in beauty, so even though she's built her own brand, she also has this wealth of extraordinary history in marketing. Up until this point, I had not really been the same age as many of the people I collaborated with in this way. I remember when she invited me out to dinner and we had a fucking blast. Nora showed me that I could be compatible relationally with the people I worked with. She helped me understand that I was no longer the "kid" trying to appeal to adults in the corporate workspace, but that I actually could be around my peers. I didn't realize how much I needed her insight to step into this next chapter of my professional and personal ventures.

I met Chelsea with *Refinery29*. She does *R29*'s Unbothered, which is a portion of their digital space that's geared towards Black women and stories, and she has produced for countless companies, including *Vice*. I knew when I met Chelsea that we would work together because she's so smart—way smarter than me—and incredibly strategic. I love being around people who can not only speak my language but also take it to another level. She has so many ideas about how to tell stories from our perspective, but she also knows how to deliver them with extreme grace.

Jeff is someone I've known the longest, from way back when I was only sixteen. He was just eighteen or nineteen and was responsible for the incredible work on chrisbrownworld.com, which was such an innovative site for its time. He's another student of the *True Jackson, VP* Effect because he was in such an adult-centric space while working as a digital publicist. Sharon was the one who found him and brought him into our lives, and he's gone on to work for the United Nations while also occupying other spaces.

At the end of the day, we're really all a group of multifaceted, talented individuals who have a drive for building innovative spaces while being a part of a larger community.

We have assisted in bringing to life so many productions that showcase a different perspective in the community. Whether that's through *The Psychological Evolution of F*ckboys*, a show about a young woman who's writing a paper on fuckboys and ends up interviewing a few different ones in order to finish her academic thesis, written by our creator Nakia Stephens; or whether it's tuning into *Live or Die*, which is a podcast hosted by Loreal Palmer and Frank Wimberley, who review horror films and discuss different themes in relation to today's cultural look at the horror genre; or whether that's *Dear Keke*, in which I speak to my audience and give them real-life advice when they phone in about their individual crises; or whether it's *Make It Make Sense*, a show in which a group of young adults sit and digest memes, from how they work, to why they're so successful, to if these memes are actually even funny underneath the surface. (Y'all, why do we love memes so much?)

It really does mean everything to give back to the world and utilize the tools I've been harnessing. KeyTV is all about creating spaces for our audience to connect and grow. We're not just talking about entertainment—we're building a community that's rooted in the real stories that create the entertainment you consume. Our goal is to create a system that prioritizes an entrepreneurial spirit, where we can incubate new ideas and collaborate with others to make something truly special. We're using digital platforms and sponsorships to make it happen, but it's not just about growth for growth's sake—it's about empowering our community to take control of their own narratives and create their own opportunities. KeyTV is built on a simple idea: when we create something together, everyone should share in the success. We're not just talking about a paycheck—we're talking about ownership and a stake in the future. As our community grows, so do the possibilities. We're not just making content, we're building a movement. And when we profit, we profit together.

We are a system that values entrepreneurship and a platform for personal and communal success.

We are KeyTV.

27

NOT A MOMAGER, A BOSS

My mother, Sharon, has always been a key part of the Keke Palmer Universe—hell, she's the one who really *built* the universe. Even still, I really do hate the stigma associated with having a mom as a manager, like how it's perceived as if they are living through their child or taking all their money, only to use it for their own fame. I think of Sharon Palmer as what she is—a Boss. I think of the ways she's created more opportunities by multiplying what's been asked of me. And throughout my career, she's asked me difficult questions about all the things I want to do and stood by my side regardless of the answer. Honestly, who would I be without her love, support, and sacrifices?

Sharon made sure she was, like me, an active learner and listener. In any room she walked into, she made sure she was asking all the questions to ensure if something was really for my benefit or for the company's. In spaces that I'm not in physically, she's been able to translate my wants and needs. She not only knows what I want, but she also knows what the people want, too.

Wherever possible, I tried to encourage my mother to step outside her comfort zone (which was usually behind the cameras) because I always felt like she not only had many things to say on certain topics, but I genuinely enjoyed her perspective on those topics. I've mentioned how much I'm trying to encourage people across generations to speak to one another to gain these different perspectives and be more open-minded.

And so I'm always in a state of awe regarding how many people are drawn to my mother's candor, which, no surprise, only speaks to one of many traits she's mastered the longer we've stayed in the industry. She's honest, she's persistent, and she knows how to have a good time when it's time to have a good time.

It was no surprise that when I floated the idea of Sharon having her own show on KeyTV, everyone was already on board. These two guys named Matt and Troy had worked with me and Lenoria on my show *That's the Gag*. When KeyTV became a thing, they pitched a show, and due to my crazy schedule, they thought it would be better if Sharon were the star. I looked at my coworkers around the table and said the fans *have* always loved her. And I wasn't seeking validation, I was affirming the truth. The truth that having Sharon at the center of this series would be an entertaining exploration of who she's been in my life and trust that Sharon would be able to deliver—even though she's typically executive producing. Enter *Bosses*.

What other series do you know that has a boss-ass older woman at the center of the narrative who is also just as funny? (I'll wait for an answer, honey.) I remember when Sharon had lines in my directorial debut, *Big Boss*, and even though it was the most lines she'd ever had in one of these videos, she really knocked it out of the park. I wasn't surprised when messages from the fans came pouring in after we premiered the first episode of *Bosses*. Someone wrote, "Now I see why Keke is so funny! 😂" Another person wrote, "I love Keke moma." Period, pooh. Comments like these do validate my desire to continue doing what I want to see as part of KeyTV while also leaning into my community around me. Yes, we could've moved in a different direction and auditioned other people's mamas in order to get this skit off the ground, but that didn't feel right to me. I remember Issa Rae's story about how, originally, finding the main character for *Insecure* was a journey, and the higher-ups were suggesting celebrities who just didn't feel true for the story she was trying to tell and portray as a young Black woman from Los Angeles. *Bosses* began with Sharon in mind and will end with her carving her own path through KeyTV.

And, y'all, while this season of *Bosses* is full of antics, it's also giving you some insight into how this business works and how you can capitalize when you have a great time.

Name a better duo than Sharon and Keke—I'll wait.

28

SHE AIN'T NO DIVA

Y'all, the music industry done tried to break me in half, in fourths, and in eighths. They didn't care that I was an artist who had a deep passion for music and singing, and they certainly didn't treat me like I had many choices in the songs I wanted to release on my own. I'm telling you, when I say "Music Industry Bullshit" is a real phenomenon, I mean it! If you want to learn something about perseverance, try letting a label play in your face today, tomorrow, and yesterday. Because I had to learn that it can and will happen if you allow yourself to be mishandled or allow for your morals to be compromised. And it's not like it's the fault of the artist either; I've talked to too many people who've felt, at one time or another, that they've placed their trust in the wrong people to lead them to something that seemed right at the time. But it really wasn't serving them as the artist, because people in the industry sometimes don't have your best interest at heart. They are simply just looking out for themselves.

Even my mother, Sharon, got caught up in the web, allowing the music industry execs to get into her head when I was younger. There was a situation where I felt forced to perform a song that I didn't feel entirely passionate about recording. I was so angry at the deceit (I'm telling you, no one is safe) that our intimate relationship was compromised for a bit because of it. But I can look back and really empathize more with my mom now more than ever before because she, like me, believed we were being looked out for by the experts in a then-unfamiliar industry. And we were only trying to build success in the medium where our love for the arts was first born. As I grew older, I found myself understanding more and more how there are certain behaviors and treatments that women experience in entertainment that just aren't fair to us. It was a deeply traumatizing experience, and I've expressed this before to anyone who knows me. I've heard similar stories from many other female artists, and I've encountered too many of these scenarios, from people telling me I should stick to acting, or wanting me to barter my body for records, or even befriending me just enough for me to let my guard down so that I could put myself in positions where I'd be taken advantage of. But you know what I did?

I just learned to step away from the situations I *thought* I had to tolerate for validity in this game and do things independently. I had to do it on my own. As much as I've talked about my feelings and my treatment in the music industry across multiple platforms, finding my way back to performing the way I do now took incredible strength.

The concept of going independent is equivalent to realizing a nine-to-five isn't working for you. It's feeling like your purpose is outside traditional institutions. It's realizing you don't want to be told what you're going to be doing every hour of the day, and you don't want to help an employer look great for their boss because you actually wanna be your own boss. So you give that two-week notice to tune in to what makes you feel more alive. You chuck up the deuces sign and walk out the doors of that stuffy, claustrophobic office with those ugly cool lights. It means sacrificing quick success for autonomy and for the freedom in choosing what works for you—not just what you are working for.

And I won't lie, taking a walk away from institutions is risky as hell. Sometimes you wanna look back because that's where your comfort zone resides. It's in the cubicle or in your corner office. It's in the consistent money (*okay!*) and the systems in place that you believed would help you achieve the next thing. But then you square your shoulders and realize that you are the most delicious thing worth pursuing and you learn that your goal isn't one with the corporation you're working with.

I've always wanted to be a hit *artist*, not have just a hit record or a hit album. But record labels need you to have hits because that's the only way *they* make money, and it's very easy in any corporate world to get their idea of success confused with yours. And before you know it, you're working to make partner to prove something to them . . . when you only ever wanted your own practice to begin with. So when you take a step back and stay in your world and not theirs, you really begin to understand that choosing yourself comes with a certain level of objectivity. And that breeds choice. And where there is choice there is freedom.

For clarity, I'm not pulling a Beyoncé in "Break My Soul" and telling you to quit your job. I am just saying you have to remember that your job isn't the be-all and end-all and not to allow yourself to get caught up in their agenda because that pulls you out of your own pursuits. Our willingness to give ourselves to other pursuits is a beautiful thing but not when it stops us from catering to our own visions. And you can 100 percent do both. For all intents and purposes my main career has always been acting. Then eventually I used my success in that career to spread out elsewhere, but what I never did was forget about those other pursuits and allow my acting success to make me believe that I couldn't still invest in other things. That investment was always predicated on money, obviously, because these things *are* expensive, but it grew over time.

So, for instance, let's say you're a designer and you work at Banana Republic. Maybe it's important to be a sales associate but not a manager because you need more money than a cashier but not as much responsibility as a manager, because you need to invest in your personal business. It's valuable what you're learning at the store, so the job is useful for what you want, but you're also staying intentional about what's important to you rather than what the company thinks should be important to you. My managers often thought acting was all I should focus on because that made *them* the most money at the time (my my *my*, have the tables turned), but little by little I would invest in music videos and show dates.

Last year I invested in a tour, which is great progress. This could be the same for my make-believe fashion designer story. You keep the job 'cause it's good and hopefully you like it enough. Make what you need to spend a little on some unique pieces for your brand and maybe do a collection by the time you're a sales associate. The point is to never let your dream die in the midst of doing the things you have to do to get what you need to invest in yourself. This is the hardest part but you are worth it.

My most recent musical venture on KeyTV has been the addition of my girl group, DivaGurl. But the creation of the group is not just purely for the music aspect; it's a culmination of many things in the

Keke Universe that includes acting, comedy, and satire, while giving nods to iconic girl groups we all loved growing up. The group is a reflection of how I'm continuing to create more storytelling through my music, which I've been doing for years. But I became more clear and intentional about it once I became more clear about myself in this industry. I love how DivaGurl is on the other end of what the music industry can feel like (aka stuffy and rigid). And this is ultimately one of the best ways I feel I can release the music I want while continuing to have fun and itching the scratch I know we all have for other girl groups.

The name DivaGurl came from a friend of mine, Lawrence, who I've worked with for years. Lawrence started off working on my street team when we were twelve for my first album. After that, he grew into directing for me and now he's creative directing this DivaGurl storyline. Lawrence has always encouraged me and my music. One day we were talking and I told him that he sees me as his "Diva Girl" and I never thought about it again. That is, until I started working on my new project and the music sounded like an old-school girl group. That was when I decided the group should be called DivaGurl. The story would be made up of four girls, who would then become three, playing off the older years of Destiny's Child. Keyana is me and she is the ultimate diva, using the DivaGurls as her launching pad to a solo career. She goes way back with Sadé, who supported the group financially, especially in the beginning, so Sadé's all business. Monét is the connection to the group's producer, KP, and eventually gets kicked out for Chantè. The two of them represent innocence, think Baby Spice. And LeShay is like Sporty Spice; she's like the rapper of the group (think Left Eye in TLC) who Keyana met in a dance group.

"S.O.B." is the first single out from the group and it was so much fun to shoot the video because it was giving me nostalgia like never before. I was having the time of my life flipping the blond ends on my bob—which wasn't stiff, honey—and re-creating choreography that a younger me would've 100 percent danced to if it played on *106 & Park* or on *Total Request Live*. And it's why it was also really special for someone like Big Tigger from *Rap City* to sit with us and create promotional content as we prepared to launch ourselves into the world. DivaGurl is always about standing and staying on business, even through the bullshit, so the songs will keep coming. And who knows? Maybe there'll be a national tour and a debut album on the horizon....

And while I love how we've been able to make space for DivaGurl through this partnership with KeyTV and Virgin Music Group, I realize that it still takes time for me to communicate my style of storytelling across my brand because I do so many things and truly believe in forging my own path, which will always make my way unique to me. I look at the Funkadelics and all the characters they created, like Sir Nose d'Voidoffunk, who existed inside the group Parliament. The narrative storytelling rooted in the story-within-a-story concept excites me. It's like when you watch a TV show and the show has another show within it. And all these things tell the ultimate story in this meta kind of way.

DivaGurl is another story within the story of Keke Palmer. Like Lady Miss Jacqueline or Chelsea Barbie Taylor or Akeelah. So it's real and also a fabrication of the stories in my storybook. I think of myself like Barbie and these are all the different extracurriculars I take part in. They're not me in totality, but they are orchestrated by me to tell the greater story of this supercreative, daring young woman who uses the world as her playground and has been supported by her family in a way that has allowed her to be brave enough to explore the deepest parts of her imagination.

Had I allowed my experience with the music industry from the past to shape my relationship to music now, I would've crushed myself into something I felt was more digestible or settled for searching for a "hit" to define my artistry. There're so many alternatives to where my path could've gone, but I kept the faith, continued focusing on the craft, and decided to build the table I'm currently sitting at the head of.

In the last year alone, I've gone on tour, performed at several universities and Pride events, and looked into a fully crowded room where people were singing my songs back to me. I've had such an amazing time because I'm learning so much about all the ways I want to evolve my shows and the different levels I can go to by adding all my different vibes into one pop. In true vaudeville fashion! Tour became not just the Big Boss Experience, but the Keke Palmer Experience. There was so much genuine music, conversation, and laughter. But most of all there was love and joy, and this love and joy is what I've always wanted to share with all the people who've forever rocked with me. I've been able to dive into a whole new level of creativity being the kind of artist that I am and will continue to be.

Entertaining is truly my transmutable medium; it's how I alchemize! It means so much to me to be able to share in that transmission from what I've found difficult in this world to something beautiful and relieving.

And, for me, the pinnacle moment this past year when I performed at the BET Awards and gave a tribute to Usher was something my dreams were made of. And to think of everything that I believe created the space for that to happen in my personal story is true alchemy. Which, I consider, is true artistry.

Of course, by now you should know that all these moments always begin with a phone call. Or a message. Most of the time the message comes through to someone on my team, so I get all this secondhand excitement from the messenger, but regardless of how I receive news that a good opportunity is coming my way, I start by thanking myself.

Like, *Keke girl! Look how far we have comeee! Love you, girl.*

This time, the message came through my manager, Big Billy Clark (who was actually my A&R and tour manager when I was twelve)! Usher would be receiving the Lifetime Achievement Award at the BET Awards in June, and I'd been asked to be part of the tribute. There were a bunch of us headlining and taking the stage to give flowers to someone I consider one of the most influential artists. From Victoria Monét and Chlöe to Teyana Taylor and Summer Walker... I couldn't (but I actually could) believe that I would be part of this special group to honor this historic moment. Which was really his historic moment.

And to think that after everything that had happened in the last year... well, you guys know. To be honest, I wouldn't change any of it. In fact, I'm a firm believer that all this happened for a reason. And while I'm definitely not saying that I was considered because of how the incident with my son's father escalated in the public's eye over my attendance at an Usher concert... But I mean, I'm sure some people were thinking it. But what it really was, for me, was an opportunity to take the stage in a way you'd never seen me before.

I've always looked up to Usher. After attending his residency in Las Vegas, I was so inspired by all the theatrical elements that make him who he is. It's like Michael Jackson was so Broadway and Usher was, too. But he didn't go Bob Fosse; he went Rosero McCoy. Rosero was one of Usher's early choreographers and when you think of Usher's style that we know today, it's like Fred Astaire but hip-hop. The dance tells a story and there's character in the movement but it's infused with so much culture and style. I related so much to what he said at his Super Bowl performance: "I took the world to the A." Me being a storyteller and centering story and character in everything I do is why I'm such a fan of how Usher shares his creations.

To perform in the midst of all that drama and maintain focus on what was important to me while showcasing what I had to offer as an entertainer with my choreographer Rosero McCoy (who choreographed the very song I dance to) onstage for his tribute is beyond alchemy! It's poetry! It was a special moment for me, my story, and my passion for the arts, and I think it's important to point out that that's not selfishness, that's simply being autonomous. No one has the right to center themselves in your dreams or try to deny you moments that are yours simply because they don't understand your story.

Talk about a full-circle moment, you know? Now the headlines about us are about our artistry. About how I, along with so many others, lit up a stage with pure devotion and love for an artist who puts his all on every stage he steps on. *Not* my personal matters—because that's not what matters. There was so much drama geared towards my relationship and a storyline that for me was so unreal considering I don't know Usher outside of being a fan. But what I wouldn't allow was for it to overshadow my true narrative as an entertainer and a true admirer of Usher, like a lot of people. To get an invite to honor someone I admire, like, this was a dream.

The BET Awards have always been known as "culture's biggest night." Which I translate to the biggest stage For Us, By Us that I've, honestly, ever known. I've been a huge fan of BET shows (y'all can't tell me nothing about *106 & Park* or *The Game*) and the awards show for as long as I can remember. And being in attendance at the awards show always feels like a huge family affair. Similar to the NAACP Image Awards. Being around community just hits different! If you know, you know!

I've always been inspired by the performances at the BET Awards.

And there are so many iconic cultural moments attached to this awards show. I remember the year when Destiny's Child reunited on BET's stage for that incredible rendition of "Cater 2 U." All the men on that stage were shook by their performance. I remember when Jesse Williams took the stage in 2016 to condemn police brutality and systemic racism when tensions in America felt like they were at their peak before the craziest election of our lifetime. And I also remember Ciara cutting it up to Janet Jackson's "Rhythm Nation" in her own tribute to a living legend. So many artists tore up the stage in their own way, and I was ready to also have my own moment where I was giving someone their flowers. That is all I ever want to do.

It was decided that it would only be right if I jumped onstage at the same time as my triple-threat brother Childish Gambino with a duet of "U Don't Have to Call." I'd memorized the lyrics to "You Make Me Wanna . . ." years ago, so performing it in an Atlanta fitted hat, sparkly jeans, and some Forces felt perfect. You can't tell me nothing; you saw the way I stepped out of those shoes?

I ate that *downnnn.*

There's a lesson here, I promise. There's something important about destiny and about speaking things into existence by living in action of what you are trying to do. About doing the work even when no one is watching or giving you your own flowers. Even though I couldn't have imagined something like this was on the horizon for me about a year ago, whether that was showing up with my DivaGurl group on the blue carpet or honoring Usher in this way, to see my love of music and performance forming this bridge together as someone who'd been slept on by the music industry in my youth is something I'll never forget. Life just surprises you, and when you stay ready, you don't have to get ready. No matter how it arrived, I carpe diem–ed.

29

KEEP LIVING

My main nucleus has always constantly revolved around three things: God, family, and entertainment. Knowing that these are the main aspects within myself, I'm able to really understand who I am and what I want to represent in the world. I know that I love God. I know I love my family. I know I like making people laugh. I know I like making people feel *good*. I want to help people and I wanna share God's light on the world the best way I can. Everything that I do becomes a way for me to express that.

And if you've been following my journey, you can see how I continue to put these core parts of my identity into practice. Whether that's through projects like DivaGurl or being a mother to Leo or sharing devotionals or acting in movies, I'm constantly moving in a way that speaks to what I value most in this world.

I would be the same exact way if I were an Uber driver! I would be in that car talking to people and having the same deep-ass, goofy-ass, five-star-worthy conversation I'm having with y'all right now! So whether it's me driving Uber or me singing at the Karaoke Lab, if I wasn't Keke Palmer, I know I would have, or create, multiple avenues for me to express who I am and what's important to me. Understanding this about myself has put so many things in perspective.

I often think about trying to find a way to bring people back to their beliefs, which is why I lean so much into my spirituality. My dad taught me the story of Jesus at an early age. How God's son died, and God watched this happen knowing that it would stand as a testament to His unconditional love for us and the ability to keep going in times of darkness. He chose to keep going. He chose to keep believing. Whether you are Christian or not, the impact of the story gives what it needs to give. Imagine if someone harmed your loved one right in front of you?

Jesus died and God had to watch it happen. But if God could give up His only son and He could still keep the world moving—especially with all the signs that he was the one true son and errrthang—I guess I can live another day! I can choose to believe, too. According to scripture, on the third day, He rose again, and to me that is the gift given in walking in your truth. Following God to me doesn't mean a perfect life, but it means rising up again whenever I fall. And this is something that helps me to keep going. To keep living. To keep believing even when things go bad.

You have to have a constant North Star. God is my North Star. For me, I always say: *Let me pray on it.* Or ask myself, *Does this align with my sense of community and what I want to represent for the community?* You have to have a rule of things that drives back to your own personal commandments. And not only should you be identifying these core values and beliefs, but you should be living them as best as you can, too. It's a North Star for a reason, but practice makes "perfect."

Take a minute to consider these questions: What is your North Star? What are your core beliefs? Can you name three things that make you who you are? And once you identify those three things, what can assist you (personally, professionally, financially) in expanding in these areas?

If you know what feels good to you, and you believe in yourself, there's a whole world of possibilities that can and will open up around you. Whether you have the faith that I have, or you're growing your faith, or you're not necessarily spiritual at all, there is at least one thing that we all feel and care about. If you're someone who loves kids and always wants kids to be happy, do you know how many jobs you can have to fulfill this purpose? Maybe you could be a teacher or work at the YMCA. Maybe you could ensure safety to kids by being a lifeguard. Maybe you see yourself participating in a Big Brothers Big Sisters program.

Identifying the things you do care about is important, but it's also equally important to create a list of the things you don't care about, what you aren't willing to do. For example, I know I'm unwilling to do things for shock value that have no real meaning to me, and I don't promote things that I don't use, respect, or agree with.

What is nonnegotiable to you? And how do you hold yourself accountable when something on your nonnegotiable list happens? Because let's be real, life be life-ing and things don't always go as planned.

Let your responses to these questions be your guiding principles. How can you use these principles to help guide you into how you choose to use all these incredible gifts that you possess as a divine human being?

Life is about living. We learn nothing by playing small and not taking risks in our daily lives, especially in our journey to fulfilling our individual purpose. My sister Loreal just came out with a memoir titled *Keep Living*, which is a phrase that's been passed down from my grandmother to my mom and from my mom to my siblings and me. What it means is that the ending can't be anticipated. We don't have that kind of foresight. And if we did, we'd never do any of the things we're meant to do. We'd never touch who we were meant to touch. Life is going to happen with or without us, so we may as well choose to live.

But it's all about awareness, action, and accountability. How bad do you really want it?

Keep going. Notice the resources that you can take advantage of around you. Take notes. Be a student while you're here and make the most of it. Be brave and be bold because why not?! And for me, my faith is a big guiding factor for why I believe there is something out there for me. But let's say that's not you and you don't have faith in that and you don't believe that the world is good or has to be good. Even on a scientific or metaphysical level, we still get to choose how we see the world. The bottom line is none of us know the truth! None of us have the answers, we all just have what we believe. So if I have what I believe, why not believe that there is good out there for me? Why not control my thoughts and form them into stories that give me the momentum to carry on? Some might call that delusional, but I call it freedom. And there is power in the freedom when you realize it's your choice to keep moving or stand still. I don't have all the answers, and it's scary to think about the lights going out until you realize that once they're out . . . it's over. The curtains have closed and there's no time for an encore. (I know, pretty dark, but I'm not sorry!) I don't know if we get an encore in our performance of being human and having this experience, so if I only get one shot, I won't miss my chance to blow because opportunity comes ONCE IN A LIFETIME! You better lose yourself! Or whatever Eminem said . . .

It's really about expressing gratitude and appreciation during the process, while surrendering to the experience of life, because the experience is all any of us know that we have for certain. We have to find joy in the skin that we're in, in the emotions that we feel, in the mini narratives and the stories within stories of our lives. And y'all, I don't know where we go after this, but I read this Eckhart Tolle book one time that told this parable about a gazelle and a lion. When the gazelle was about to be eaten by the lion, it got scared. But once it was torn apart, the gazelle realized that it was all a dream. Let's live the dream even if we experience a brief nightmare because in the end, we wake up! We're a different person from when we entered the dream before.

I turn back to my faith and think about God, how He created us and why. For me, it's the story and the ideology of God because I see it as both science and spirit. Meaning there is space and time and there is also the spirit who created them. There is Jesus, the son of God, and then there is the actual sun that lights up the world. There is the time where the sun went down and we lost the light and all the things that allow growth, but then it came back. The telling of our world and our people are also magical tellings of just atoms. It's all how you look at it. I think that's what faith and growing up in the church did for me. They showed me how to find the glory. How to choose to see life as an empowering story and not just a bland existential thingamajig. It's poetic, but if we strip it down without a narrative, then there is this mass of nothing. That was so lonely, it creating something and that creating something else, and so on and so forth. Narratively speaking, God so loved the world that He created His only begotten son. What that means to me is God is this energy that created the universe, the earth, and all the planets and was so lonely. God then created us and so on and so on. It's this idea that the energy kept growing, and the poetic telling of that is so it wouldn't be alone, and that's kind of why we all create. To experience community, whether creatively for work or with a family or whatever. We as humans are a reflection of that mass that I call God. That mass can exist without us but we cannot exist without that mass. That said, we share this inherent loneliness. Which is why we keep creating. Which is why we search for experience with one another.

And this is why my parents emphasized the importance of community to me, because it's all we have in our lonely existence. All we have in our mass is each other. And all God has is us, and the desire to share that beauty with one another that existing as a being gives you the opportunity to experience is, to me, worth living for.

30

JACK OF ALL TRADES, MASTER OF ME

I was having a conversation with a friend the other day about what it means to create a foundation that will allow you to fulfill different aspects of yourself. We talked about how people thought going digital would not be helpful to me or my career. They didn't see the vision I shared and were ready to write me off in a way that felt, frankly, disheartening—especially since I knew that my belief in myself was greater than anything anyone could've ever told me. I was reminded that people will always have 101 opinions about the way you should live your life. They will try to tell you who you are, but the secret is:

You don't let other people tell you who you are. You tell them who you are.

I always go back to that Marianne Williamson quote: "Our deepest fear is not that we are inadequate. Our deepest fear is that we are powerful beyond measure." (We used it in *Akeelah and the Bee*, and this woman's quote has been misattributed to Mandela for almost twenty-five years! Sorry to that woman!) Essentially what she's saying is that once we admit that we know who we are, or that we're awesome, then we've got to *do* it.

Don't be the person who's holding you back. My mom used to always say, "Keke, you always carpe diem. You just carpe diem." And even though I knew what it meant, I never really understood that this was something that people didn't do. You telling me you don't carpe diem? Because, honestly, the reason why I did, and continue to do, is because I don't feel like I have another choice.

If I don't do x, and if I'm not living x, then in my mind, it's like I'm dying. So I do it.

When I was a child, my dad whooped my ass whenever I lied. From an early age, I knew I've got to say what I mean and mean what I say. I learned that I could not go back on my word. The core of who I am is already built to do what I said I was going to do. And I apply that to discipline. The concept of discipline that is important to me, and that assists me in getting to my goals, is knowing that now that I've said it, I've got to do it.

And if you live as this authentic version of yourself, then how could you lose? When I die (and the nonbinary, body-positive individual starts to sing), I can take that last breath with ease knowing those who knew me really knew me. Through this discipline and consistency in building my brand, I also learned that having this entrepreneur mindset is the way of the future; this is our way forward. Being an entrepreneur means having autonomy in the workforce and choosing what you want to do. Sometimes even the idea of being an entrepreneur can feel far-fetched, but you don't realize how attainable it actually is. You shouldn't just want to focus on working your way up at a big company. You should want to figure out what you can learn from said company and take that to something else you're more passionate about.

My friend, a fellow millennial, made a great point. He said, "We're also growing up in a generation of uncertainty because we've seen all these lies revealed so there isn't a lot of trust in the system."

I don't disagree. In fact, I'm definitely of the mind that we've entered society with such an acute and amazing point of view that now we have to dust all the debris off to get our strength back. The reason why so many of us are struggling with the mentality that we're struggling with today is because we're living in an outdated system. This system tells us that we're supposed to live the way Gen X and the baby boomers did when, actually, we're the people who are here to pioneer a new wave. We're actually not trying to do all this corporatism bullshit. We are now birthing a new way of existing, which is *I have five jobs and then I'll tell you when I want to get back to you.*

But because we're the ones creating it, we don't really know if it's the right thing. There will be trials and errors that we'll have to figure out on our own terms. That's why parents and guardians are so quick to ask questions like, "You're doing something different already?" and "When are you going to just stick to something?"

Not everybody has a Larry and Sharon who, when I wanted to try my foot at something different, were like, "Shit. Do whatever you want Monday, Tuesday, Thursday—just commit." A lot of people are dealing with their parents saying that they've got to find something—which is typically just *one* thing. And it's like no, first of all, that's not possible! 'Cause one thing is not going to pay my bills (by the way). Number two, guys, I can't live the way y'all live.

There is no judgment but we are supposed to raise new questions and push things forward. There's too much going on and we've got to create autonomy within the workforce for ourselves; otherwise, they're going to kill us and tell us that we enjoyed it.

Corporations have gotten too huge for us to work with only one and find an ounce of happiness, because it's clear they can't care about us and their business at the same time. It's no longer feasible to focus on becoming the person they need us to be, and maybe it never was.

So what now?

Make YOU your career. Master yourself. The freedom of choice is what makes any of us feel like we have purpose! And choice is often taken in the workplace and in our family units, still I found liberation in mine. And this book is meant to assist all people, but especially my fellow millennials, to understand that what you envision is possible and it's what I live.

Everyone of every age has to understand that the career is you and the job is the place you go to support YOU. That's the only way we can control the pace of this hamster wheel. I can't tell you to get off 'cause I don't know that I want to. But I hope these tools can tell you how to find comfort in it! Remember that you are not on anyone else's timeline, only your own. The only thing you have to do is follow through. It doesn't matter who doesn't love it or get it, it matters that you do. And before we can expect anyone to validate or legitimize what we are doing and putting our time into, WE have to. As I mentioned before, I've been met with resistance when stepping into different spaces, but I didn't let other's confusion about me become my own. In the words of Sharon Palmer, "You just *commit*" and I did. I have with every single thing I've done. I've committed!

So to any of you reading this book, just commit to your dreams, commit to YOU. Follow your North Star, fall down and get back up, use one job to pay you to learn the skills you need to help you get to level three on your game plan, meet partners, friends, and collaborators who also care about what you're doing. Follow the LOVE, create a community, and have FUN on your journey. Because if you're gonna be here, at least make it something to write home about. Don't play small!

The truth is I've heard the phrase *jack of all trades, master of none* all my life and it used to feel very discouraging. I felt like the people who had said it either had been crushed and pushed into one thing or were truly far too inhibited. It never made sense to me that you couldn't be great at many things. Or the idea that you needed to be a master at everything. I couldn't articulate it but to me it's about mastering you. Of course there is mastery in a skill but there is always more to learn. If we master our ability to be unafraid and try new things, to switch lanes and be flexible, then why would there be anything we can't master? The hardest thing is not mastering skills but mastering oneself. To me the phrase is a fraud and a lie because if I've mastered my mind, honey, I'm unstoppable!

And if I have mastered my mind and remain in the business of mastery, then I am open to things in a way that others may not be. The freedom I feel is what I want to continue to share. My perception and how I choose to control my narrative and view my life are exactly what make me successful. But someone else without this skill would say I'm delusional, or that I'm hiding my misery, or that, actually, I'm only financially successful and not successful in regards to love or family. Those are all reflections of their inner monologue. If they're saying that to themselves, then they could never understand what I say to myself. This is the sad part; I wish everyone could choose a better inner dialogue because what we think truly is what is.

Glass half-full or half-empty?

I found out while writing and thinking through this book about the history of the saying, which some attribute to William Shakespeare. The full quote is "A jack of all trades is a master of none, but oftentimes better than a master of one." I was gagged! So I continued to dig and found even more tea! So get this—the idiom that inspired *jack of all trades* was not attributed to anyone. Then a version of it was used as an INSULT toward Shakespeare via a hater named Robert Greene, and during the Industrial Revolution, the literal *master of none* piece is adopted, of course.

The plot thickens! So the original idiom was socially created and then changed as the times changed to encourage maybe a more industrial mindset. It's assumed that *oftentimes better than a master of one* was Mr. Shakespeare's contribution, but there is no actual evidence of when, or where, he said it. *I'd* like to imagine it was his clapback to Mr. Greene. Or maybe it's the collective consciousness having a Mandela effect moment—where we have all decided that there is not as much power in focusing on one industry as there is in focusing on one's self. Whether he said it or not, Shakespeare was not only writing, producing, and directing his shows, but oftentimes even building the stages! He knew that being capable of all things requires self-mastery, while mastering one thing—no shade or no tea—simply just requires focus on one thing. He got some haters for it, but all in all, I'd say he was winning! It doesn't call you to look inside yourself and pull from a different place; it doesn't necessarily equip you for change. Being open to learning and having multiple skills forces you to evolve in a way that shouldn't be missed. Like my sister always says about Lacan and his theories on language and how it impacts our understanding and ability to relate to one another. Language and phrasing and cultural definitions are always changing! And we have the power to put meaning behind something and decide what power it holds, just like we have the power to define ourselves.

That's the epitome of mastering me. In my need to change, to survive, to be flexible, to find joy, to be stretched and pulled, I learned how to master myself in this world as a woman, a millennial, an entertainer, a Black American, a MOTHER, and so on and so on. And that doesn't mean it's finished, but now that I have the tools, no matter what changes come, I am equipped to deal with them. I can't control the circumstances of life, none of us can, but if we can just control ourselves and shift ourselves and be—again—like water, we can always alchemize and make purpose out of pain. You know? We gotta be able to be flexible, 'cause it's never gonna go our way. It don't matter what you do. Life is about having fun and enjoying, but I believe it's also about working hard. It's important to work harder and smarter, and work harder for the benefit of yourself. If that benefits others, too, that's great, but this is why we have to be intentional because time is what we are buying.

"Mastering Me" means that you get to write your own story. A lot of times I don't think our experiences and how we were raised allow us to believe that. My parents did what they did uprooting our lives and chasing dreams to show us we had that choice. No matter how it all turned out, on the most basic level, they wanted us to know we have options and ways to see the world. I want people to understand that the power is not in what is happening, but how we choose to see it. Circumstances are always a tough thing. They are!

It's terrible! I've had really tough years between the ages of twelve and seventeen, and then twenty-one and twenty-four, and then a really, *really* tough year between twenty-eight and twenty-nine. And I have had many tough days in between. Things have happened to me, but I refused to let my life stay in the genre of drama or horror, and I know I have the choice to actually make my life a deep romance or a comedy.

Life is all those things, and it's important that we don't get too caught up in the performance without realizing that we are also the writers. Turn the page!

There is power in your presence.

The last few years have brought us into a new world—the rules are completely different, and not enough people are talking about how to operate in our new systems and current culture.

I would like to use my life as a case study to help people see how to leverage their personal power into major power. It doesn't matter how little you have; what makes you different is your currency. I figured out my power was in diversifying. People told me to stay in my own lane, but I realized that to diversify is power and that my talent was putting my fingers into different buckets, that way no one could control me. They said, "Jack of all Trades, Master of None." I said, "No, I *am* the Master of Me."

And that is what I want for you. To find your personal power, grow your self-esteem, and find your enjoyment in life. To find power in managing this world by centering your desires and letting that guide you to what you need to do to slice the life you want for you. There is a way to get there and this, well, this is my strategy.

There is so much more to learn. At twenty-one I wrote my first book and learned that I didn't belong to other people's ideas of me. That I could quiet all the voices I didn't want to hear, that didn't serve me, and I could move to the beat of my own drum. Well, now I'm doubling down on that at thirty-one and saying not only do I know how to quiet outside voices, but I know how to control my own. I know how to tell myself what to believe in, what not to believe in, when to let go, and when to hold on.

I learned how to find joy when all there was was sadness. I learned that I'm in control and that who I present to the world and how I am perceived are based on the way I've mastered me.

MASTER OF ME
SELF-ASSESSMENT EXERCISE

1. **Where is purpose most likely to emerge?**
   a) Around rich people
   b) When pursuing material success
   c) When in a state of comfort, safety, and ease
   d) When meeting others' expectations

2. **What drives purpose?**
   a) External recognition
   b) Financial gain
   c) Passion and inner interest
   d) Social media likes

3. **Where does purpose reside?**
   a) Outside us, waiting to be discovered
   b) Within us, waiting to be discovered
   c) In our job title or career
   d) In our relationships with others

4. **How do we express purpose?**
   a) By trying to meet others' expectations
   b) By conforming and looking to society
   c) By trusting our inner guidance and intuition
   d) Through external validations

(Answers on the next page.)

ANSWER KEY

1. ANSWER: C) WHEN IN A STATE OF COMFORT, SAFETY, AND EASE

REFLECT: What makes you feel most at ease and comfortable? How can you create more space for this in your life?

COUNTERACT: One of the greatest indicators that something isn't meant for you or shouldn't be part of your journey is persistent discomfort. This isn't about shying away from challenges, which are a natural part of growth. Pay attention to your inner wisdom and distinguish between challenges that fuel your growth and those that drain your energy.

2. ANSWER: C) PASSION AND INNER INTEREST

REFLECT: What activities make you feel most engaged and motivated?

COUNTERACT: When in apathy and fear of having nothing you're truly engaged with, try things. Create a personal game plan to get your hands on any and all things and most of all be patient and kind to yourself in the process.

3. ANSWER: B) WITHIN US, WAITING TO BE DISCOVERED

REFLECT: What are the things you did as a kid that came naturally to you? What are things you like to do when you are alone?

COUNTERACT: Shy away from believing what you love on the surface has to be the "thing." The thing is to be followed and will constantly evolve. It's the source of the feeling you're harvesting through following what feels good.

4. ANSWER: C) BY TRUSTING OUR INNER GUIDANCE AND INTUITION

REFLECT: How often are you following your negative and critical thoughts? How would you respond if you heard your friend talking to themselves the way you speak to yourself?

COUNTERACT: A great guide to finding your true voice is to realize it isn't all the crazy mean thoughts going on in your head. Filtering through the projection means choosing not to believe the negative thoughts and instead planting something more positive because that's the real you. The you who's choosing, not just accepting whatever debris exists externally.

OPEN-ENDED QUESTIONS

Here are some probing questions to help you discover moments of purpose and understand what being purposeful feels like. Get out your journal and let's get into it!

- Think of a time when you felt fully engaged and motivated. What were you doing? What made it so fulfilling?
- Recall a moment when you felt like you were making a meaningful contribution. What was it about that experience that made it feel purposeful?
- What activities make you lose track of time? What are you passionate about that makes you feel fully alive?
- How do you feel when you're doing something that truly matters to you? What emotions arise?
- What would happen if you released the need for your purpose to be achieved by a certain time or age?
- How would you approach your purpose if you knew it was a journey, not a destination?
- What small, incremental steps can you take today to move closer to your purpose, without feeling pressured by a specific timeline?

KEY TAKEAWAYS

- Purpose emerges in comfort and ease
- Purpose is within us
- Trust your inner guidance
- Purpose is a feeling

Acknowledgments

I'd like to thank my family. For always encouraging me, showing me what love is, and teaching me most of all how to love myself in this crazy, complicated world of human imperfections! I thank them for the foundation that they gave me, which makes me feel like they will always be with me no matter where I go.

I want to thank my best friend, Lenoria Addison, for always being here as a friend and an inspiration. Knowing her is a pleasure, and working with her is a gift. She is everything I ever wanted in a friend! Like right out of a storybook, and the spirit of our friendship and what we have learned together is all through this book.

Thank you to Lacy Lynch, my book agent, for being in my life all these years! I have known you since I was twenty-one, and you have always understood my voice and encouraged me to keep speaking and sharing what I know, even when I think there's nothing

ACKNOWLEDGMENTS

there. You have always assisted me and helped me craft my voice as an author, and I'll never know how else to say thank you outside of making you as much money as possible. Also thank you to your team, Haley Reynolds and Dabney Rice.

Thank you to my book publishers at Flatiron, Megan Lynch and specifically Kukuwa Fraser. This book wouldn't be what it is without you. Your guidance and your walking hand in hand with me through this journey has been a pleasure. I have also looked to you and taken your constructive criticism and wit as a guideline for all the people I hope would want to pick up this book. You are all the things I admire and hope others could see in me.

And a huge thank-you to Sharon Palmer, Max Wyeth, Jeff Lopez, Chelsea Sanders, and Tevin Giddens for being an integral part of my KeyTV team. Also thank you to Billy Clark, Dave Becky, Luke Dillon, and Cari Davine for believing in and collaborating with me on the Keke Palmer brand. You all are amazing people who equally have your hands in so many things. But you choose to work with me and assist me in my mission, and I could only hope that you know my success is equally your success. There is no way I could alchemize in this way without your love, support, and brilliance! Thank you for being my community.

About the Author

KEKE PALMER is an Emmy Award–winning actress, singer/songwriter, host, producer, author, and passionate voice of the millennial generation. She rose to prominence at age twelve through her breakout role in *Akeelah and the Bee*, starring opposite Angela Bassett and Laurence Fishburne, and has gone on to star in more than twenty-five films and thirty TV shows. Most recently, Keke starred in Jordan Peele's Universal Pictures summer blockbuster *Nope* and hosted NBC's reboot of *Password* with Jimmy Fallon, which had the most-watched new, unscripted series premiere of the summer across the broadcast networks. She is the CEO of KeyTV—a digital network dedicated to spotlighting a new generation of diverse creators and democratizing the entertainment industry—and the record label Big Bosses Entertainment.

"With my luck, I'll come back as myself."